BROWN BOOZE

TAKE 5 KEY SPIRITS, MAKE OVER 75 DIFFERENT COCKTAILS

MICHAEL BUTT

DOG 'N' BONE

Published in 2013 by Dog 'n' Bone Books
An imprint of Ryland Peters & Small Ltd
20–21 Jockey's Fields   519 Broadway, 5th Floor
London WC1R 4BW   New York, NY 10012

www.rylandpeters.com

10 9 8 7 6 5 4 3 2 1

A CIP catalog record for this book is available from the
Library of Congress and the British Library.

ISBN: 978 1 909313 15 6

Printed in China

Editor: Clare Sayer
Designer: Geoff Borin
Photographer: Martin Norris
Illustrator: Steve Millington aka Lord Dunsby

For digital editions, visit www.cicobooks.com/apps.php

CONTENTS

Introduction 4

Brown Booze Essentials

The Recipes

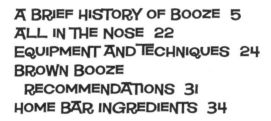

INTRODUCTION

During the early years of producing distilled alcohol the name "water of life" was used to describe this wondrous new creation, giving an idea of the reverence and amazement the early distillers and consumers had for its near-magical properties. This phrase survives as *aqua vitae* in Latin, *eau de vie* for the spirits that are blended to make cognac, *akvavit* for Scandinavian schnapps and even *uisge beatha*, the Gaelic word for whiskey.

This fascination with distilled alcohol survives to this day, with aged spirits continuing to gain new fans and advocates all across the world. But when you start out on this voyage of discovery the huge number of brands, categories, styles, and prices can be very forbidding. What do I choose? And once I have bought something, what do I do with it? Many of us will have encountered self-proclaimed experts who say things like "never put ice in Scotch" or "cognac should be gently warmed," and are generally dismissive of those who don't follow their rules. Many of us will also have recoiled at the first sip of strong alcohol; consuming spirits neat is not the best way to begin to experience their glory, but the end goal is that you become adept at appreciating the nuances and qualities of these spirits.

This book will give you plenty of information to demystify the different styles of aged spirits, helping you to enter the world of the booze connoisseur. Brown booze simply refers to five key "brown" spirits: North American whiskey, Scotch and Irish whiskey, rum, brandy, and agave spirits. But, more importantly, this book answers the question, "what do I do with it?" The old cliché of sipping spirits by the fireside is very limiting, and I hope to show you that brown booze can be just as versatile a drink as vodka or beer. There is nothing to fear from making brown booze cocktails and this book will show you how easy it is. With over 75 simple recipes, using little else but a few bottles (which you probably already have in your drinks cupboard) and some standard supermarket ingredients, the world of brown booze will become a lot less mysterious and a lot more fun. Happy mixing!

BROWN BOOZE ESSENTIALS

A Brief History of Booze

Alcohol has been enjoyed in some form or another for around 4,000 years. What follows is a brief explanation of its journey to the present day.

TWO DRUNK MICE
The early history of alcohol from prehistory to the water of life

Alcohol is a gift from nature. Leave ripe fruit in the sun, and with the right conditions and the help of beneficent microorganisms, potable alcohol is created. In fact, there is evidence of higher primates and even elephants taking advantage of this, deliberately leaving whole trees of fruit to ripen and then taking advantage of this natural fermentation to have an end-of-season party.

The microorganisms are yeasts: a huge family of invisible helpers, without which there would be no leavened bread, and certainly no beer. Alcohol is a by-product of their life cycle, as enzymes—or organic catalysts—convert sugars of all descriptions into alcohol and carbon dioxide. The CO_2 makes the bread rise, the alcohol makes the party. It is difficult to know exactly when humans discovered the effects of alcohol and learnt how to adapt and control the natural process for their own ends. What we do know is that the very earliest civilizations left containers that were almost certainly used to hold and store

alcoholic beverages, and some of the earliest writings, whether on wax or stone tablets or on papyrus, were about booze.

Probably the nicest story comes from Mexico. Legend has it that a shepherd was minding his flock when a great storm came, scattering his animals. The shepherd took shelter underneath a rock to wait out the storm. The morning after, he began searching for his sheep. Near to his hiding place, where he had seen a particularly large bolt of lightning, he came across an agave plant riven in two and charred from the strike. The agave plant was vital to the livelihood of his people, giving them food, fuel, and a fiber for sewing and making ropes; in fact the plant was so revered that it was considered a manifestation of the mother goddess Mayahuel.

At the base of the split agave he noticed two mice licking the sweet nectar that was dripping from the wounded plant. It was clear that they were enjoying it immensely; as he approached the mice ran away in a dazed manner, seemingly reluctant to leave. His curiosity piqued, he tried a little of the liquid, and a little more, and a little more. Later in the day he staggered back his village—without his sheep, but with a huge smile on his face. He had discovered Mother Nature's most lasting gift—alcohol.

Production of fermented alcohol continued throughout the world, often with methods unchanged since prehistoric times. The next stage in its development was distillation—essentially a simple process of separation. Alcohols boil at different temperatures from water; ethanol—the one we are concerned with—boils at 78.4 degrees Celsius. Distillation is simply a method of using this characteristic to separate the alcoholic component of a liquid. The history of distilled alcohol is somewhat shrouded in mystery but we can assume that the ancient Greeks understood the concept of differential evaporation, and may well have used it to concentrate wines more than 4,000 years ago. After the fall of the classical civilizations much knowledge was lost, and with it definitive proof of the use of distillation for drinking purposes. The technology resurfaced with the rise of the cradle of civilization in Persia. Consumption

of alcohol was prohibited but the pursuit of scientific endeavor certainly was not; our numbering systems and much of our knowledge of astronomy were developed here. Alcohol is an excellent organic solvent, capturing and preserving a wide range of aromatic compounds and acting as a carrier for pigments. The techniques of distillation were probably perfected in the quest to produce perfumes and cosmetics—the word alcohol comes from the Arabic *al'kohl*, meaning essence. The word alembic (used to describe the simplest type of still) also comes from this period. This knowledge of distillation spread and reached Western Europe sometime around the eighth century AD. From there it spread slowly north, with the technology usually disseminated alongside Christian teachings, leading to the characteristic distilled spirits of Europe. Indeed, the names given to distilled alcohol—*aqua vitae*, *akvavit*, *eau de vie*, *uisge beatha*, and even vodka—demonstrate both this connection with monasteries and the church and a deeper belief that distilled alcohol was a "Gift from God."

MISSISSIPPI MEANDER
The discovery of maturation and the birth of brown booze

All spirits come off the still looking the same—clear and colorless. However, to transform spirits into the ones discussed in this book there is one vital step: maturation. People had been storing distilled spirits ever since they made more than could be drunk in a single day, but strangely it was left to the New World to develop the process that makes booze brown— prolonged contact with slightly porous oak. In the Old World spirits were often stored and transported in stone or earthenware flagons, essentially inert containers that

were sealed carefully to stop any evaporation or spillage. Over time any liquid containing organic compounds will develop, even in the absence of oxygen; in fact, we rely on this to allow wines to develop in the bottle (although there is a tiny amount of gaseous exchange through the cork). People often call this mellowing, and it is a great thing to try at home with your favorite cocktails. Make a Manhattan and bottle it up carefully in a sealed container. After one month the flavor will be quite different, with various elements in the flavor profile more thoroughly integrated; after three months the effect will be more pronounced; and after a year it will have changed in appearance (although you may not be able to leave it that long!).

The story of this momentous discovery is one of a local preacher and amateur distiller in Kentucky by the name of Elijah Craig. Most of the settlers in pioneer America were refugees from war, famine, and taxation in Europe, with the most adventurous being those of Scots and Irish descent who crossed the Appalachians to settle in Kentucky and Tennessee. They knew about making whisky from back home and many had brought their small stills with them, so as they as they pitched up they began to make whiskey. Very quickly they adopted the native maize as a suitable raw material and began to produce whiskey in the sort of quantities that they could sell. The only problem was that they had no customers; the only large markets were the new big cities growing up on the Eastern seaboard, and the mountains they had crossed to reach their new lands were difficult to carry any volume of cargo over. Their only option was to ship it downriver to New Orleans, where it could be taken by sea up to New York. Legend has it that Elijah Craig had some barrels that had been used previously to transport fish. Then, as now, barrels were expensive, and being a canny Scot he decided to burn the wood that had been in contact with the fish, removing the smell. This process of charring the barrels, unknown to him, concentrated the vanillins and tannins in the layer just below the char. He sealed up the barrels and shipped them downriver. The Mississippi was only navigable in the summer months, and

the three-month journey in hot conditions proved the perfect way to accelerate the process of spirit entering and leaving the wood every day, taking with it the aromatic compounds from the oak, and leaving behind some of the heavy fusel oils and impurities. When the casks were opened, the liquid inside had turned from clear to amber and was immediately noted for its smoothness and exceptional taste. Whether the story is true or not, the whiskeys from Bourbon county in Kentucky quickly became famous, and brown booze was truly born.

FROM FIELD TO FLAGON
How do you make brown booze?

The process of manufacturing spirits can often seem like an arcane and almost random one, but in fact all distilled spirits follow roughly the same pattern in their creation. The wonderful diversity comes from very subtle differences and changes that occur in the five basic elements of making brown booze: raw materials, fermentation, distillation, filtration, and maturation.

RAW MATERIALS

The most important ingredient in liquor (aqua vitae) is also the most important ingredient in life: water. In a standard bottle of spirits, more than half the content of the bottle is water added at some point after distillation. This means that it plays a massive part in the final taste of a product.

Not all water is the same—although the minerals found in mineral waters come from a reasonably small set, the flavors can be quite different as the mineral level and type defines the water's physical and chemical properties. Water is used in two ways in the production of liquor: it is used to produce the original mash and is also added after distillation.

The production of ethanol in all alcoholic products relies on the fermentation of sugars through the action of yeast. The different raw materials that provide these sugars will affect the final product.

The action of yeast, or more specifically the enzymes, called ferments, can be described by the simple equation below. An enzyme is simply an organic catalyst and as such remains unchanged through the reaction.

$$C_6H_{12}O_6 \rightarrow 2C_2H_5OH + 2CO_2$$

Glucose → Ethanol + Carbon Dioxide

There are generally four sources of sugar found in materials used for potable alcohol production. These are:

Natural sugars Found in all fruits and the basis of the production of alcohol in brandy.

Grain starch The energy source for the germination and early life of plants before photosynthesis occurs. These form the basis of the production of whiskeys.

Plant starch The starch held in mature plants as energy storage. This can be subdivided into root stores (sugar beet), tubers (potatoes), and stem storage (agave).

Sugar cane A fast-growing grass with a very high sugar content in its sap.
Each of these sources requires different processes to prepare for fermentation and should be treated separately, even though the end product can be very similar.

Fruit

Any distilled alcoholic beverage that has its basis in fruit can be defined as a brandy. However, there are two distinct types of fruit used: those that contain a high enough concentration of sugars to ferment unaided, and those that require the addition of sugar to start the process.

Unaided fermentation Grapes, stone fruits (apricots, peaches, cherries, plums), apples, and pears

When one thinks of brandy one automatically thinks of grape brandies (the word comes from the word *brandewijn*, meaning burnt wine). Grape

wine was certainly the earliest consumed product of fermentation (although mead and beer were close behind). Grapes ferment easily because of their high sugar concentration and the fact that their skin provides a convenient home for yeasts. The spread of the vine has been based on this happy coincidence alone.

Even within this category the source of the fruit sugar makes a great difference to the end product—think of the difference between wine and cider or cognac and calvados. Fruit variety also plays a part—the difference between Pisco and cognac is primarily down to the use of different grapes; Pisco generally uses muscat grapes, known for the production of sweet wines, while cognac uses ugni blanc grapes, which make thin, acidic, dry wines. This acidity means that the wines it produces are low-strength and not considered to be particularly fine, but conversely it produces brandies of unrivalled complexity.

Stone fruits are used in the production of several spirits, the most famous being Kir or Kirschwasser (cherries) and Slivovitz (sljiva plums). In many of these brandies and liqueurs the stones of the fruits are used as well, bringing a characteristic bitterness to the final product.

Aided fermentation Raspberries, strawberries, black and redcurrants This is a much smaller category, both in terms of production and of consumption. The most widely drunk is probably framboise eau de vie. Sugar is added to the fruit to raise the concentration that can support natural fermentation. This should not be confused with liqueur production, the technique of macerating fruits in high-strength alcohol and then distilling the product.

Grain

The catch-all term for the seeds of grasses (ranging from small rye seeds all the way up to maize), these are the storage devices of the embryo of the new plant. The mother plant stores energy to aid the initial growth stages of the offspring. This is stored as insoluble starch, to allow the seed

to remain dormant for a time without degradation. Unfortunately for the production of alcohol, this insolubility of starch is a major issue.

Producers get around this with a process known as malting, which relies on the fact that the plant must convert the starch to sugar for its own purposes. The grain is first soaked and then kept at the correct temperature for germination. If the conditions for growth are correctly mimicked, the enzymes in the grain begin to convert the starch. This process is then halted by heating the plant, just as it begins to produce a shoot and the starch has all been converted. The grains are then ground up, ready to begin fermentation when suspended in water.

Malted grain used to be the basis of all grain-based spirits and is still used in Scotch and Irish whiskies, and as a starter in the manufacture of bourbon and other American whiskies. However, the production of vodka uses a different method: adding artificially produced enzymes to milled grain, which produces the same starch-to-sugar reaction.

Malting prepares the grain for fermentation, but in Scotch malt whisky the process also adds levels of flavor. With Irish whiskey, bourbon, and other spirits, malting is done with indirect heat, often steam, whereas in malt whiskies the malt comes into contact with elements of the fire and smoke. This toasting process changes the flavor, depending on how heavily toasted the grains are—this is used a lot to change the flavors of beer. However, in Scotch whiskies the biggest effect comes from the grain coming into contact with smoke from the peat fires, and this peatiness, or "peat reek," can be detected even after distillation.

Different types of grain will produce completely different spirits—even in vodka the differences between rye, wheat, and barley are pronounced. Probably the best example of this is American whiskey, where the mash bill (the ration of grains used in the production) plays a large part in the final taste of the whiskey. The four main grains used in spirit production are:

Barley Used for Scotch and Irish whiskies and Finlandia vodka. Most bourbon whiskies are around 10 percent barley.

Wheat Used for Absolut, Stolichnaya, and many other Scandinavian and Russian vodkas, as well as some bourbons.

Rye Used for Wyborowa and most Polish vodkas, straight rye whiskey, Canadian whiskey, and as a component of most bourbons.

Maize All bourbon and Tennessee whiskey must be at least 51 percent maize. Corn whiskey and some vodkas, such as Skyy, also use maize.

Plants

Some plants store large amounts of starch in parts of their systems to allow them to grow more effectively. There are generally two types: plants that have their starch stores underground, such as root succulents (sugar beet or turnips) and tubers (potatoes and yams); and those that store their starch above ground.

Potatoes are used in the production of characterful vodkas from Poland, where one particular variety, Stobrawa, is used. It has a very high starch content to maximize the yield of usable sugars. Sugar beet is generally used to make neutral spirit for the lower end of the market, and for the production of industrial alcohol. The transformation of starch to sugar with potatoes and beets is a more simple process, based on breaking the long-chain starch molecules with heat. The product is "cooked" in an autoclave or steam oven; the softened pulp is then ground and mixed with water to form the basis for fermentation.

The plants that store their starch above ground are leaf succulents. By far the most obvious and common example is the agave used in Tequila and Mescal production.

Sugar Cane

Sugar cane is a fast-growing grass of the genus *Saccharum*. There are several species used for the production of rum, but all are defined by the very high sugar content of their sap, which can reach concentrations of up

to 10 percent (gomme syrup is only 50 percent). This makes it a great raw material for distillation, as it can be used immediately. The cane grows very quickly and in the tropics can grow all year round, with new areas coming to maturity all the time. This means that rum production is not nearly as seasonal as that of other spirits, which are mainly produced in temperate regions and rely on storing raw material for winter production, or, as with Cognac, closing the distilleries during certain times of the year.

Sugar cane is used in different ways to produce three main styles of rum:
Cachaca The national spirit of Brazil is produced from the whole cane. This is the simplest treatment of the product.
Rhum agricole Produced in the French Caribbean, most notably Martinique, it uses the free-running juice of the sugar cane.
Rum Often known as English-style rum, although it includes Cuban and South American styles as well as rum produced in the British Caribbean. Rum is produced from molasses, a by-product of the manufacture of sugar.

FERMENTATION

The process of fermentation occurs naturally—the word is often used to describe the process of fungal respiration, both anaerobic and aerobic. Yeasts are fungi, and the process of fungal growth is harnessed in many areas of food production, from blue cheese to yoghurt to sauerkraut.

The production of alcohol requires a more specific definition of fermentation. It is the anaerobic respiration of sugars without oxidation to form an alcohol and carbon dioxide. Essentially, fermentation is the name given to the chemical conversion of sugar into alcohol and carbon dioxide, using naturally occurring yeasts. Different strains of yeast will have slightly different effects, and when they react with more complex sugars and sugar sources, different alcohols and other aromatic organic compounds will be created. The reaction is limited by the amount of available sugar but also the hardiness of the yeast. Above a certain level of concentration, alcohol will kill off the yeasts.

Emil Christian Hansen at the Carlsberg Brewery in Copenhagen undertook further study of yeasts in the late 19th century, and was the first to work out that naturally occurring yeasts are made up of variant strains of the organism. He is credited with the first monoculture strain (*Saccharomyces carlsbergensis*), but more importantly he led people to understand the benefits of using cultured yeast—as opposed to naturally occurring strains—for both yield and consistency. These days brewers and distillers will carefully select and store their strain of yeast for its desired effects.

There are two types of fermentation, aerobic and anaerobic, and they are responsible for the different aspects of flavor. These are often described in beers as "top fermenting" and "bottom fermenting." They produce different chemicals, ranging from acids to aldehydes and aromatic esters, and vary wildly in the speed of fermentation. Most spirits undergo 40–50 hours of fermentation, but many ferment for as long as a week. The length of time is determined by the ratio of top fermenting (quick) and bottom fermenting (slow) yeast action.

DISTILLATION

Distillation is the process of purification through the action of heating a substance to a gaseous form and then selectively condensing the required component. There are other forms of separation that are used in the production of alcoholic drinks, most notably freeze concentration—used in the production of Applejack—whereby an alcoholic mixture is concentrated by allowing it to freeze and removing the ice (water).

If the process was as simple as separating water from ethanol, it could be done accurately in a simple still with just one distillation, up to an accuracy of 96 percent pure. This is the maximum purity achievable in RTP (room temperature and pressure) distillation, because water and ethanol form an azeotrope, meaning that at a certain point the mixture retains the same composition in its vapor state as in its liquid state.

Pot distillation

The pot still is the original form of still and is used for the production of some brands of almost all types of spirit. The style of modern pot stills came into use in the sixteenth century, with the use of copper. A still is divided into three parts: the kettle or base is the vessel where the liquid is heated, the neck or swan neck is the hurdle over which the vapors have to travel, and the lyne arm or line pipe is the path to the condenser and collection vessel.

The fermented wash or mash is placed in the still and then heated. As the liquid starts to vaporize the resulting liquid is collected. This first distillation occurs in what is known as the wash still. It takes a distillate from 7–9 percent alcohol—produced from the fermentation of the raw materials—up to around 21–29 percent. These liquids are known as low wines.

These are then placed in a second still, sometimes called the spirit still, and are re-distilled. The results of this second distillation are separated into three categories: the heads or foreshots, which contain high alcohols and aromatics and are recycled back into the system; the heart, the spirit that will actually be used; and the tails or feints, generally also re-distilled or discarded. The hearts of the distillation represent around 20–30 percent of the total run, and it is the art of the distiller to pick his cut points to gain the best flavors. The liquid coming off the second distillation will vary between 52 percent (tequila) and 70 percent (whiskey and cognac) alcohol by volume (ABV). Some distillers, most notably in Ireland, distil a third time. This allows a lighter and purer spirit of around 80 percent ABV to be produced.

The pot still requires artistry of the master distiller, and is both labor-intensive and time-consuming. The continuous still came about to get around both of these points.

Continuous Still

A continuous still is a double columnar device to take the guesswork and inefficiency out of the production of spirits. The system is designed to allow exact fractions to be removed from a sample, automatically reducing the need for an experienced master distiller. Because the process runs continuously and can be recharged, the inefficiency of a stop-start operation is removed.

Most people consider the use of the continuous still to be primarily for white spirits and grain whiskey. However, because you can choose the level of accuracy and define a range of fractions, other spirits, including Armagnac and most bourbon, can come from a style of continuous still, just at a lower proof.

FILTRATION

Filtration, or the removal of unwanted material, is the easiest way to improve the quality of a wine or spirit.

There are two types of filtration: mechanical and chemical. Mechanical filtration works very much on the principle of a household sieve. Water and ethanol are small molecules, whereas much of the contaminant matter that would occur in a sample of alcohol would be much bigger. Mechanical filtration can remove these simply by making the filter "holes" smaller than the unwanted chemicals.

One of the easiest ways to construct this level of filtration is to use a compacted system of granular material to act as the sieve. This approach can be seen across the production of white spirits, from the use of quartz sand by Bacardi, flint in Siberian vodka, diamond dust, etc. The choice of material matters little. All that is important is the fact that it is inert and very fine. Mechanical filtration is often promoted as an important part of the manufacture of many modern premium and super premium vodkas, with many dubious statements used to give uniqueness to this essentially mundane procedure.

Chill filtering is another process that is commonly used to filter spirits mechanically. The solubility of a liquid changes with its temperature; the colder a liquid is the less soluble material it can hold, and the ability for larger molecules to remain in suspension is reduced. This material will then sink to the bottom of the vessel where it can be removed. This is most commonly used to remove tartrates from whiskey, although some would say that chill filtration reduces flavor in this case.

The other, and far more important, type of filtration is chemical filtration. This is used to remove specific unwanted chemicals. The earliest known examples of these were used in the fining of wines. They were used to remove sediment by coagulation of the material followed by gravity-based filtration. This addition of a fining agent works well for wine, but the molecules in spirits are in smaller concentrations, making chemical fining an expensive process.

In the 1870s a chemist working for Smirnoff in Moscow noted the effectiveness of activated charcoal for filtration. He had, of course, invented nothing new—alchemists had been using charcoal for hundreds of years—but his development was how to market a thoroughly filtered alcoholic beverage.

Charcoal efficiently absorbs some hydrocarbons while acting inertly to most minerals. Technically, absorption is not a chemical reaction, as both the carbon and the impurity remain unchanged, but it acts as one because the bond between them removes the chemical from active circulation. This process is vital in the chemical industry as well as in the production of spirits. Filtration can be split into three areas:

Filtration of water supply All spirit manufacturers have to filter their water supply to a certain extent; the differences occur depending on the availability of a clean water source. Distillers ensure a consistent and clean water both to add to the distillation process and for reducing to bottling strength. Most manufacturers go to the expense of deionization to ensure consistent mineral levels and to rule out the risk of any corrupting environmental pollutants being added.

Filtration before aging This is a rare process as most filtered spirits are un-aged, but there is one notable exception. Tennessee whiskey is characterized by the Lincoln County Process, which accelerates the production of a smoother whiskey by filtering it through sweet maple charcoal.

Filtration before bottling The process of charcoal filtration before bottling is all about making the spirit as fine, smooth, and pure as possible. Multiple filtrations are often used with a combination of mechanical and charcoal methods.

MATURATION

One of the most magical aspects of alcohol production happens in the months and years after distillation. Raw new-make spirit is often known as Moonshine and is a harsh and uncomplicated product. It is placed in oak barrels, to emerge after a period of time as a brown, mellow, and complex spirit.

The process of barrel aging has been known about for hundreds of years, but understood for far less. The first drinks to benefit from this extra aging were probably wines and fortified wines taken aboard ships on the earliest voyages to India and the Far East. These wines were kept at the bottom of the hold as ballast and consumed throughout the voyage, and it is certain that some difference was noted between the first sip and the last. Unfortunately, storing a product before sale costs the producer money, and so the concept of improving wines and spirits in this way did not immediately catch on. It took until the late seventeenth century for European commerce to be stable enough to have merchants stocking maturing spirits, as well as a market that would consume them. The brandies of Cognac were possibly the first to be recognized as benefiting from their time in wood, with whiskey and rum following very soon after.

Barrel aging is a mysterious process relying on a variety of variables. Aging in wood allows for four things: oxidation of aromatic chemicals in a slow and controlled manner; change in alcoholic strength from

evaporation; filtration; addition of flavors from the cask itself. All four of these processes are happening in every stored barrel of spirits in the world, but it is the varying degree of each process that creates the astonishing variety of final tastes. There are a number of factors which contribute to the aging process:

The type of wood A barrel can be made from anything, but oak has always been the most sought-after material. This is because it is hard and durable, but not so hard as to be inflexible or too difficult to work. It is also plentiful and has a natural resistance to decay when properly cured. Within the large oak family there are specific types that are more desirable, but whichever variety is used will change the characteristics of the whiskey and also the speed of aging. Scotch manufacturers are now experimenting with the influences that the different types bring.

The size of the barrel Barrels go from 60 liters all the way up to nearly 1,000 liters. Spirit aged in a small barrel has more contact with the surface of the wood and therefore gains aged characteristics more quickly than spirit in a larger barrel.

The age of the barrel Barrels can theoretically be used again and again. The first fill, however, will gain more influence from the wood and have more filtration effects from it than subsequent fills. Bourbon manufacturers can use their barrels only once, but other types of spirits can use older barrels that influence both the speed of aging and also the amount of sweet wood compounds and oak tannins that enter the spirit.

The degree of char or toast When the cooper is making the barrels he heats the staves over a fire to give them the flexibility to bend into the correct shape. This char creates a thin layer of active charcoal and also concentrates the sweet wood compounds in a layer just beyond the char. Cognac and sherry manufacturers traditionally only lightly char their barrels, and then re-char to refresh them when maintaining them through the life span. This extends the barrels' life to many even fills. Bourbon

manufacturers char much more heavily as they want to fully access the vanillins and tannins in the oak. These differences in char change the speed of aging but also affect the color and taste of the spirit.

The climate The concept of effective wood aging relies on the expansion and contraction of spirit into and out of the wood, caused by temperature change. A large change in daily temperature brings on the quickest aging, so whiskeys aged in temperate but hot climates age faster than tropically aged rums, because the difference between day and night temperatures is greater. In Scotland, however, aging is very slow as the temperatures are lower and temperature change is smaller.

The conditions of aging The size, location, and style of the aging house can have an effect on the aging process both by influencing the local microclimate (even to the level of different areas of the warehouse) and also the level of efficiency and waste. The "angel's share" is the spirit that evaporates away during aging, and the levels of this are defined not only by temperature but also by local humidity—the more humid, the smaller the loss. Retaining humidity therefore is a good way of reducing waste, but also means that the temperature in the closed system will have less variation. Manufacturers need to consider this balance to gain the correct compromise. Other strange effects can occur because of the location of the aging houses, particularly if they are near the sea or in windy locations—the whiskies of Laphroaig gain their salty character from wind-blown salinity.

The length of time This ranges from as little as a couple of months in some tequilas to half a century in some malt whiskies and cognacs. Most experts agree that there are optimum ages for different spirit styles, but as all the other effects are so variable the rules are made to be broken. Everyone agrees, though, that there is a level above which wood flavors begin to dominate and produce acrid notes in the final spirit.

All in the Nose

HOW TO TASTE AND ASSESS LIQUOR

The most difficult skill in technical bartending is certainly training the senses of smell and taste to become tools; we have an amazing olfactory system, capable of distinguishing ingredients as diffuse as 5ppm (parts per million). But where do you start? Everyone has the ability to connect sensations with remembered things, times, and places. That is why when you first smell a spirit or wine you may find the things in your head are not necessarily just about food. The first thing you need to do is interrogate your palate, trying to discern the different elements that make up the taste profile. These will, in the beginning, have little outside reference; they are your thoughts, after all. The next step is to start to build taste profiles more in terms of the whole product. This is needed to truly grade and identify compared spirits. This is all really hard and can take a lifetime to answer. The longest journey starts with a first step.

When tasting beers, wine, and spirits it is good to take a systematic approach to recording the results. It not only makes directly rating and comparing spirits easier, but also allows you to compare products tasted at different times.

TASTING

• The first taste is with the eye—look at the bottle if you can. This will give you a reference to its ABV and how that influences the spirit. It will also give you a ballpark idea of tastes to expect.

• Now to the product—again use your eyes. Firstly, is it free of foreign bodies? These generally mean that the product might be corrupted and tasting worthless. Now on to the color. There is a huge range of specified colors used in tasting, but you can make up your own. The color can tell you a lot about certain products, giving clues about aging, depth of flavor, or additives. It is most useful when comparing similar products.

• Swirl the wine or spirit—look how the liquid returns to the level, leaving

characteristic trails or legs (tears). These can give a good idea of the relative viscosities of liquids. In spirits long legs mean high sugar, high alcohol.

• Swirl again to release the aroma—this requires a tasting or wine glass to ensure the aroma is contained. Here is the first major mistake—DO NOT stick your nose in and sniff! The alcohol will completely desensitize your nose for about ten minutes. Gently approach the glass until the first aromas are apparent; retreat and then slowly proceed to get closer. It is often said that if you breathe through your mouth close to the glass, the aroma will travel up the back of the nose (this does work!)

• Assess the aroma—light and fruity, zesty, or more complex? Are there any obvious flavors that you can identify, and is there a dominating flavor, or is it more balanced?

• Now for the taste—be careful here: there is no need to take in much liquid, since we don't want to desensitize the mouth either. Generally, the best way is to place a small amount on the tongue and let it heat up and evaporate as it moves around the mouth. Remember you have taste buds all around your tongue, so make sure the spirit passes around the mouth.

• Assess the taste—to do this it is easiest to split it into sections: initial, mid-palate, and mouth feel. These can show how the spirit develops after you get the primary taste. Remember, smell is just able to access the airborne component of the drink, and these most volatile flavors are often the lighter notes, while the deeper undertones will arrive when the spirit has warmed up in the mouth.

• Balance is key—as with everything in life. The spirit should have a round and full profile with discernible character. The mouth feel is also important. Does the spirit fill the mouth or taste a bit thin and watery? Even when tasting vodkas, mouth feel is probably the biggest clue to what is going on.

• The finish—this is not just the burn when the spirit passes down your throat. You don't even have to swallow. Finish is more about the lasting impression you are getting from your senses. Is the finish pleasant or harsh? How long is it? Some cognacs will have finishes lasting tens of minutes.

• The reassess—if you are tasting comparatively then you should always go back to anything you are unsure about, as you will set boundaries and comparisons with the other examples. One brandy might have hints of apple, as might another, while another still might have more prominent pear flavors. Without checking back, accurate comparisons can't be achieved.

• The process is always a learning one. The best way is to design a system to record your tasting notes in a permanent manner, in a style that is consistent across all the tastings you do. You will find that you will quickly build quite a reference guide and also a vocabulary of taste to work with.

Equipment and Techniques

You can make cocktails almost anywhere, and there is no need to spend a lot of money on fancy equipment. If you look around your kitchen I bet you will find at least ten specialist items you never use, from fondue sets to bread makers, mandolins, and the clever little gadget for cutting the top off a boiled egg. Cocktails can be shaken in Kilner jars and vacuum flasks, strained with a pasta fork, and stirred with a pencil (pencils actually make the coldest martinis), but if you are even remotely serious about making drinks at home it is worth assembling a set of basic bar tools. They will make your life easier and your drinks better.

GLASSWARE

The majority of the drinks in this book can be served in one of five glasses:

Cocktail glass Sometimes wrongly called a martini glass after its most famous occupant. The standard size is around 7oz (200ml).

Rocks glass or large, short whiskey tumbler
Often called a double old-fashioned glass, of around 12oz (330ml).

Highball glass A tall glass that can hold around 14oz (400ml) of liquid.

Wine glass This versatile glass is one that most people should already have in their collection.

Irish coffee glass
This glass comes with a handle, which is why it's often used for hot drinks.

If you are making drinks only for yourself, then it is perfectly acceptable to buy just one of each, but hopefully with your new-found mixology skills your company will be much in demand and therefore it is sensible to buy a set of matching glasses in each category. Buy glasses that you like, and look after them. Wine aficionados will tell you that glass shape and rim thickness have a large impact on how a wine "presents" and it is true, so try and get good ones. Note that cocktail glasses in particular vary massively in size, so larger ones may require some adaptation of the recipes—and a tougher liver.

GARNISH TOOLS

"The first sip is with the eye" is all too true—a well-made drink can be made amazing with just a little care and some artistic finishing touches. Most garnishes are made with a knife (see page 30), but there are a couple of cheap tools that can make it much easier to deliver perfect-looking cocktails.

Canelle knife Often known as a zesting knife, this tool cuts a thin ribbon of zest from a citrus fruit that can then be knotted or made into a spiral. If you want to make slightly larger citrus twists to finish your drinks, a good-quality potato peeler works very well.

Fine grater Used to grate chocolate, cinnamon, or nutmeg at the last minute to release the aroma of spices. It is worth buying a good-quality laser-cut grater as the old-style punched-steel box graters are much less effective.

Cocktail sticks and toothpicks You can, of course, just use wooden ones, but for a little *je ne sais quoi* consider getting a set of decorative cocktail sticks. Available in glass, steel, or even silver, they are not expensive and really make a difference. Just make sure they are long enough to work with your chosen glassware.

STRAINERS

There are three types of strainer used to make cocktails, the most important of which is the hawthorne or variable strainer. As with all strainers the purpose is to separate the drink from the ice and any solid components of the drink.

Hawthorne strainer Consisting of a perforated plate with handle and a spring, most designs allow the two pieces to be separated for easy cleaning. To use a hawthorne strainer, place it in the top of the tin of the Boston shaker (see page 28), spring inwards. Your finger should fall naturally on the small tab in the centre. When straining drinks over ice the drink can then be simply poured into the glass. When straining drinks that are served straight up, push the tab on the strainer downward to compress the spring, making the apertures between the coils smaller and removing any small shards of ice that have been created while shaking.

Julep strainer Originally designed to keep fragments of mint inside the glass when drinking a mint julep, this tool is fantastic for pouring stirred drinks from the Boston glass. It allows for a smoother pour, with no spillage. Simply place the strainer inside the glass at a 45-degree angle, hold the handle steady by wrapping the index finger around it, and pour.

Fine strainer Similar to a tea strainer but with a larger gauge mesh ($\frac{1}{16}$in/1mm), this strainer is often used with a hawthorne strainer to remove completely any shards of ice or small fragments of fruit and herbs that might spoil the appearance of the drink. To use, place the hawthorne in the Boston tin as normal and pour the liquid through the fine strainer into the glass.

SHAKERS

The most important piece of equipment for producing cocktails is obviously the cocktail shaker. There are two main categories of shaker, although as they have always been seen as decorative items there are thousands of different designs, from the simple to the outright bizarre. Antiques fairs, flea markets, and of course the Internet are great places to find interesting and beautiful variations.

Standard shaker The original shaker basically has three parts—a tin, a straining cap, and a lid. These shaker sets are used more rarely now as the compression seals between sections have to be highly engineered and therefore expensive before they work properly.

Boston shaker These became more popular in the late 1940s. The Boston shaker consists of a tempered-glass mixing vessel and a stainless-steel tin. This is the tool most professional bartenders choose, as it gives the most flexibility and is quick to use. It is a little harder to master than a standard shaker but certainly worth the practice.

To use a Boston shaker first place all the ingredients in the glass half. This gives you a useful secondary check on your measuring. Next fill the glass with ice; the amount used will affect the dilution of the drink so it is important to be consistent. The easiest way to do this is always to fill it to the very top. Next place the Boston tin on top of the glass and press down gently. The ice inside will very quickly chill the air, causing it to contract and form a seal between the two halves. You can check the seal by picking the shaker up by the tin. The glass should be stuck to it.

Shaking requires effort! Holding each half of the shaker in each hand, shake as hard as you can for 10 seconds, the idea being that the ice and liquid travel from one end of the shaker to the other, crashing against the ends, mixing the liquid while chilling and diluting it.

To open the shaker, reverse the position so the tin is on the bottom, grasp both halves in your non-dominant hand and gently tap the protruding brim of the metal half with the heel of your hand to break the seal. If it doesn't break easily, try rotating it 90 degrees.

PREPARATION TOOLS

Most of the work in making cocktails comes before the shaking—prepping your ingredients and measuring. Many of the tools required are already in your kitchen, but there are a few extras you will need.

Bar spoon Used for two purposes: stirring drinks and layering. Layering has two approaches: for non-mixable spirits such as Kahlua the flat end can be rested on the surface of the liquid and the ingredient poured gently down the stem of the spoon. For more troublesome combinations, such as Baileys and Grand Marnier, it is better to rest the bowl of the spoon cup side up and pour the liquid into this to slow the flow right down.

Spirit measures Throughout the book the recipes are defined in parts, to save any confusion with different measuring systems. A part can be anything from a spirit measure or a shot glass to an egg cup. It is worth buying a set of professional spirit measures, either in multiples of ounces or 25 milliliters. They make measuring half parts much easier and allow you to use corresponding measuring spoons for small quantities. It is also useful to have a graduated measuring jug for larger quantities, especially if you are making drinks for friends.

Muddler This is simply a stick for crushing fruits and releasing the essential oils and aromas from herbs. You can easily substitute a rolling pin without handles for this purpose, but if you are planning to make a lot of fresh fruit drinks, a proper muddling stick with engineered points or ridges will make the process easier and faster.

Juicer You will need a juicer for any drinks using citrus juices. Any style is fine; some food processors come with an attachment or you can buy an electric one for not too much money. I still like to use a hand juicer for most cocktails, but if you are making drinks for a party it is easier to go electric. NEVER buy pre-juiced lemon or lime juice—they all taste disgusting.

Knives These are often overlooked but they are the most important piece of equipment, and the one that takes the most time to master. Most bar knives fall into two categories: serrated and plain-bladed. Serrated blades are very useful for cutting citrus fruits, as the sawing motion will easily cut through tough skins. Also, for preparing citrus twists a serrated blade is much better for pith removal. Straight-edged blades are more useful to a bartender in dealing with softer fruits and where a particularly fine edge is required.

When using any knife make sure you have a cutting board to protect you and your surfaces. This allows a firm base to any cut stroke. If you are having difficulty cutting round fruits, cut a section from the end to form a flat and stable base. A good bar knife should be a 4–6in (10–15cm) long, flexible-bladed paring knife. The only time you may need a bigger knife is to cut watermelons or large pineapples. When cutting large objects use a knife big enough that you can see the tip and the heel all the way through the cutting stroke.

Any knife you use must be very sharp, so keep a sharpener to hand. Sharp knives not only make nicer-looking garnish with precise edges, but are also easier and quicker to use. In the event of an accident, injuries from sharp knives are usually less severe because less driving pressure is required for the cutting stroke. Most, however, occur because of carelessness or misuse. You get only one set of hands, so take care of them. Take your time and practice until you feel comfortable.

Extras Once you, and more importantly your friends, have realized that you like making cocktails, there are a number of other tools that are worth purchasing. Consider investing in an egg-white separator, a pineapple corer, an olive/cherry pitter, a crushed ice maker, and a large insulated ice bucket to complete your home bar set-up.

Brown Booze Recommendations

When faced with the huge range of potential purchase in the liquor store, it can be easy to get a little nervous, particularly when parting with your own hard-earned cash. Here are some brands I guarantee will not disappoint:

AMERICAN WHISKEY

Maker's Mark: Maker's is a wheated bourbon, with no rye in the mashbill. This makes for a more approachable taste and a hint of sweetness, making it perfect for drinks with fruit.

Woodford Reserve: With a relatively high rye content and substantial time spent aging, Woodford is a complex but very balanced bourbon, perfect for making Manhattans (page 42).

Wild Turkey: Using some of the most heavily charred barrels in the industry brings pronounced vanillins and upfront oak character to Wild Turkey. With this and its hefty ABV it works well in citrus-based drinks, particularly the Whiskey Sour (page 45).

Jack Daniel's: No mention of American whiskey would be complete without Jack Daniel's. The charcoal mellowing process produces a spirit that pairs perfectly with maple in a St Lawrence (page 51).

SCOTCH & IRISH WHISKEY

Johnnie Walker Black: A full-bodied blend with plenty of oily character and some smoke makes for a versatile cocktail whisky. Great in a toddy (page 70) or a Scotch Collins (page 66).

Home Bar Ingredients

The first mistake people make when setting up a home bar, or even just planning a cocktail party, is going to a liquor store and buying lots of booze, which then just sits unused in the drinks cabinet, gathering dust and oxidizing. The best spirits to buy are obviously different types of brown booze, and strong spirits do not noticeably deteriorate if kept properly. There are, however, some staples that are worth buying and keeping in stock; you never know when you or your guests might fancy a cocktail.

IN THE LIQUOR CABINET

Orange liqueur: A vital ingredient in lots of cocktails, a good-quality orange liqueur will allow you to make great rum drinks, margaritas, and much more. I would recommend always having a bottle of Cointreau in stock, as it will also work in all the recipes that require triple sec or orange Curaçao. If you love rum drinks though it is definitely worth getting an orange Curaçao. Pierre Ferrand makes the very best, but any brand that bottles at 35–40 percent will be of good quality. Some brown booze drinks work well with aged orange liqueurs like Grand Marnier, so if you fancy picking up a bottle it will serve you well. As a bonus, good orange liqueurs can be enjoyed on their own with a bit of ice.

Angostura bitters: There has been an explosion in the number of aromatic bitters available to buy in recent years, with lots of companies across the globe producing a variety of styles, based on almost every type of ingredient you can think of. Although not the oldest, to my mind the best is Angostura, made in Trinidad and Tobago. With its immediately recognizable packaging it is an absolute requirement in every commercial bar and should also be in every home bar. By all means experiment with other styles of bitters—visits to a good cocktail bar will enable you to try some of the more esoteric ones. Buy a bottle if you like them—they don't deteriorate and are normally sold in small sizes.

BOURBON, RYE & TENNESSEE WHISKEY

Drink	Simple Syrup	Lemon Juice	Angostura Bitters	Lime Juice	Egg	Cream	Soft Drinks	Liquor Cabinet	Store Cupboard	Fresh Ingredients
Manhattan p42			✓					Vermouth		
Boulevardier p43			✓					Campari, Vermouth		
Apple Manhattan p44								Apple liqueur, Vermouth		
Whiskey Sour p45	✓	✓			White					
California Sour p46	✓	✓			White		Orange juice	Orange bitters		
Nebraska Sour p47	✓	✓			White			Merlot		
Old-Fashioned Old-Fash. p48			✓						Sugar	Orange
Modern Old-Fashioned p49			✓						Sugar	
Old-Thymer p50		✓	✓		White			Orange bitters	Sugar	Thyme
St Lawrence p51	✓								Maple syrup	
Whiskey Smash p52	✓	✓ (wedge)								Mint
Devil's Share p53	✓	✓ (wedge)					Orange juice			Orange, ginger
Louisiana Jam p54	✓								Apricot jam	Mint
L 'n' G p55	✓	✓						Chambord, Cointreau		
Harvest Moon Punch p56	✓	✓					Apple juice	Cider	Cinnamon, star anise, clove	Orange
New York Flip p57	✓				Yolk	✓		Port		

SCOTCH & IRISH WHISKEY

Drink	Simple Syrup	Lemon Juice	Angostura Bitters	Lime Juice	Egg	Cream	Soft Drinks	Liquor Cabinet	Store Cupboard	Fresh Ingredients
Rob Roy p60			✓					Vermouth		
Auld Lang Syne p61			✓					Drambuie		
Blood and Sand p62			✓				Orange juice	Cherry liqueur, Vermouth		
The Weegie p63		✓	✓				Pineapple juice	Cointreau, orgeat		
Apricot Old-Fashioned p64	✓		✓				Orange juice	Orange bitters	Apricot jam	
Honeyed Irish Old-Fashioned p65							Soda water		Honey	
Scotch Collins p66	✓	✓					Soda water			Orange
Penicillin p67	✓	✓			White					
Marmalade Sour p68	✓	✓			White				Marmalade	
Raspberry Sour p69	✓	✓			White				Raspberry jam	
Whisky Toddy p70		✓							Honey	
Irish Coffee p71						✓			Coffee, sugar	
Irish Apricot Flip p72					Yolk	✓			Apricot jam, honey	
Raspberry Blow Fizz p73	✓									

SUBSTITU...

Many cocktails ...
an ingredient ...
number of drin...

GLASSW...

For each of the ...
the following k...

Cocktail

G INGREDIENTS ⟲

be transformed into another drink simply by switching
. Just follow the arrow symbol above to maximize the
u can make from the ingredients you have to hand.

ktails, a particular style of glass is recommended. Use
o identify the right glass to choose:

Collins & Highballs

Rocks

Wine

Irish Coffee

INGREDIENTS CHART

This chart will help you quickly
establish the cocktails you can make
based on the ingredients
you have at home.

BOURBON, RYE & TENNESSEE WHISKEY

There are four main types of American whiskey: bourbon, rye, Tennessee and Canadian. The cocktails in this chapter use mainly bourbon, rye, or Tennessee whiskey.

KEY POINTS TO NOTE

• The story of American whiskey is intimately connected with the birth of the American nation. Fleeing from taxes in the east for the offer of land, settlers moved west and south to the meadows of Kentucky and began to grow maize as a staple crop. Excess corn was distilled to make whiskey— which was almost as good as a currency back then. The limestone-filtered water was ideal for distilling—and the whiskey was all the better for it.

• The mashbill, or ratio of grains used, has a significant effect on the character of a whiskey. The majority has to be corn but the rest can be made up of a combination of three grains: barley, rye, and wheat. Each brings its own character to the spirit and the recipes are normally a guarded secret. Rye tends to bring peppery notes; wheat a softer, sweeter flavour.

• Legend has it that the process of barrel-charring that has such an effect on the character of bourbon was discovered by accident by Elijah Craig. He had a particularly odious barrel that he wished to transport whiskey in so he decided to burn the inside of the barrel to remove the smell. After the journey down the Mississippi to New Orleans it was noted that the whiskey had taken on both color and flavor. The science behind this is simple— charring draws the natural sugars and vanillins in the oak into a layer just below the surface of the char, from where they are drawn into the bourbon.

• The laws surrounding the production of American whiskey are some of the strictest governing any type of alcoholic beverage. The full list for bourbon is as follows:

1 Bourbon must be made from not less than 51 percent corn and not more than 79 percent, otherwise it is classed as corn whiskey. Rye whiskey must be made from at least 51 percent rye.

2 Bourbon must come off the still at less than 160 proof, or 80 percent alcohol by volume (ABV), to make sure that grain character is retained.

3 Bourbon must be aged at no more than 125 proof (62.5 percent ABV). This ensures that the producer allows sufficient contact with wood. It is cheaper to age at higher proof as you need fewer barrels.

4 Bourbon must be aged in new charred American oak barrels. These four words ensure that the bourbon has the best chance to age quickly.

5 Bourbon must be aged for at least two years; and any fewer than four must be stated on the label.

6 Bourbon must be bottled at not less than 80 proof or 40 percent ABV.

7 Bourbon must be made in the USA.

8 Rye whiskey and Tennessee whiskey tend to follow all these rules to the letter apart from one: there must be nothing added and nothing taken away. The charcoal filtration in Tennessee whiskey is deemed to do this, therefore it cannot qualify as a bourbon.

• Tennessee whiskey—and one brand in particular—has taken over the American whiskey market. At the repeal of prohibition whiskey makers needed to get up to speed and onto the market quickly, but making good whiskey takes time. Jack Daniel's patented the Lincoln County Process, where the bourbon is filtered through 12 feet of maplewood charcoal. The process gives it a maple sweetness but means it is no longer a bourbon.

• When appraising bourbon it is important to note that the absence of additives means that the color is a true representation of the aging of the product.

• The aging in Kentucky is some of the most extreme in the world. The barrels are brand new and therefore full of flavor. The temperature changes that occur during the summer months drive the bourbon by expansion into and out of the cask at a massive rate.

• In most cases rye whiskey tastes similar to bourbon, and indeed its aging is very similar. There is, however, a pronounced dryness with spicy notes through the palate. Rye whiskey suits Manhattans and New Yorkers perfectly.

MANHATTAN

The original Manhattan was made with rye whiskey and the slightly spicy flavor works well. If no rye is to hand, bourbon makes an excellent substitute — softer and slightly sweeter. This is often known as a "West Coast" Manhattan because of its more laid-back nature. Try altering the proportions slightly to your taste, and the particular whiskey and vermouth being used.

TYPE: STIRRED—STRAIGHT UP   **GLASS**:

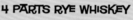

4 PARTS RYE WHISKEY
2 PARTS SWEET VERMOUTH
2 DASHES ANGOSTURA BITTERS
GARNISH: TWIST OF ORANGE ZEST,
COCKTAIL CHERRY

Stir the ingredients over ice and strain into a chilled cocktail glass. Squeeze the orange twist over the surface of the drink and discard. Garnish with a cocktail cherry.

↻ Switch up the rye for Scotch and you have a Rob Roy (see page 60).

BOULEVARDIER

The Negroni is one of the world's greatest drinks, made with gin, vermouth, and Campari. This Tennessee whiskey version is just as fantastic and makes a great aperitif or sundowner drink. Feel free to adjust the level of Campari to suit your taste, as it is quite bitter.

TYPE: STIRRED—ON THE ROCKS   **GLASS:**

3 PARTS TENNESSEE WHISKEY
2 PARTS SWEET VERMOUTH
2 PARTS CAMPARI
GARNISH: ORANGE SLICE

Stir all the ingredients with ice and strain over fresh ice into a large whiskey glass. Garnish with a large slice of orange and serve with a stirrer or spoon.

APPLE
MANHATTAN

This Manhattan variation works best with a light bourbon whiskey, although it still tastes great using rye or Tennessee whiskey. The key is not to use a poor-quality apple liqueur; these can generally be recognized by their lurid green color and artificial aroma. If you can find it, Berentzen's is my favorite.

TYPE: STIRRED—STRAIGHT UP **GLASS:**

4 PARTS BOURBON
1 PART SWEET VERMOUTH
1 PART APPLE LIQUEUR
GARNISH: APPLE SLICES

Stir all the ingredients over ice and strain into a chilled cocktail glass. Garnish with 5 thin slices of apple arranged into a fan shape, notched, and placed on the rim of the glass.

WHISKEY SOUR

This is one of the world's most widely popular drinks due to its drinkability and the fact that it works with any whiskey. The egg white can be omitted but its inclusion brings a wonderful lightness of texture to the drink.

TYPE: SOURS—ON THE ROCKS   **GLASS:**

5 PARTS AMERICAN WHISKEY

2.5 PARTS LEMON JUICE

2 PARTS SIMPLE SYRUP

2 DASHES ANGOSTURA BITTERS

1 SMALL EGG WHITE

GARNISH: ORANGE SLICE OR LEMON WEDGE, COCKTAIL CHERRY

First shake all the ingredients without ice to emulsify the egg white. Shake again with ice and strain all ingredients over fresh ice into a large whiskey glass. Garnish with an orange slice or lemon wedge and a cocktail cherry.

CALIFORNIA SOUR

This drink is a fresh variation on the classic whiskey sour; it works best with lighter American whiskeys and even better when the sun is shining. Use freshly squeezed orange juice, or at least purchase good-quality not-from-concentrate juice.

TYPE: SOURS—ON THE ROCKS   **GLASS:**

5 PARTS AMERICAN WHISKEY

3 PARTS ORANGE JUICE

2 PARTS LEMON JUICE

2 PARTS SIMPLE SYRUP

2 DASHES REGAN'S ORANGE BITTERS

1 SMALL EGG WHITE

GARNISH: ORANGE SLICE

Shake all the ingredients without ice to emulsify the egg white, then shake again with ice. Strain over fresh ice into a large whiskey glass and garnish with a slice of orange peeking up through the foam.

NEBRASKA SOUR

This great drink uses a typical Californian merlot to dovetail with the rye whiskey, but other American whiskeys and wines will also work. A great drink to finish the last bit of a bottle of wine.

TYPE: SOURS—ON THE ROCKS   **GLASS:**

- 4 PARTS RYE WHISKEY
- 2.5 PARTS LEMON JUICE
- 2.5 PARTS SIMPLE SYRUP
- 1 SMALL EGG WHITE
- 3 PARTS CALIFORNIAN MERLOT

GARNISH: NONE

Shake all the ingredients, apart from the red wine, without ice to emulsify the egg white. Shake again with ice and then strain over fresh ice into a large whiskey glass. Gently pour the red wine through the foam and swirl before serving.

OLD-FASHIONED
OLD-FASHIONED

The Old-Fashioned was created in The Pendennis Club in Louisville, Kentucky, adding sugar and flavorings to soften and smooth the whiskey. I have updated this only slightly, removing the flesh of the orange, as most of the whiskey available today doesn't need to hide its light under a bushel.

TYPE: STIRRED—ON THE ROCKS **GLASS:**

2 COCKTAIL CHERRIES
2 STRIPS OF ORANGE ZEST
1 SUGAR CUBE
5 PARTS BOURBON
2 DASHES ANGOSTURA BITTERS
GARNISH: 3 CHERRIES

Muddle the cherries, orange zest, and sugar cube in the bottom of a large whiskey glass. Add a little bourbon and stir, then add ice and the remaining bourbon, stirring continuously until the level of liquid and ice reaches nearly to the top of the glass. Garnish with three cherries speared on a cocktail stick.

MODERN
OLD-FASHIONED

This is one of the great ways to enjoy whiskey—the drink continuously evolves as more ice melts and more sugar dissolves. Feel free to reduce the amount of sugar or try different aromatic bitters. Just remember that with a great whiskey not much of anything but the water from the ice is needed.

TYPE: STIRRED—ON THE ROCKS   **GLASS:**

1 SUGAR CUBE
5 PARTS AMERICAN WHISKEY
2 DASHES ANGOSTURA BITTERS
GARNISH: LARGE ORANGE TWIST

Crush the sugar cube with a dash of the whiskey and the bitters in a whiskey glass. Add ice and the rest of the whiskey a little at a time, stirring continuously until the liquid reaches the required level. Thoroughly express the zest from the orange twist and add to the glass. Serve with a stirrer or spoon.

OLD-THYMER

Adapted from a recipe by cocktail guru Jamie Stephenson which won an international whiskey competition, this take on the Old-fashioned brings an extra dimension to the world of whiskey on the rocks. The thyme brings out interesting flavors not normally noted in whiskey. For an even more citrussy creation try using lemon thyme.

TYPE: STIRRED—ON THE ROCKS GLASS:

2 FRESH THYME SPRIGS
1 SUGAR CUBE
1 DASH REGAN'S ORANGE BITTERS
5 PARTS BOURBON
GARNISH: LARGE LEMON TWIST,
FRESH THYME SPRIGS

Muddle the thyme with the sugar cube and a dash of bitters in a large whiskey glass. Slowly add ice and bourbon, stirring continuously, until the liquid reaches the required level. Squeeze the lemon twist over the glass and add to the drink with a few extra thyme sprigs.

ST LAWRENCE

For a lighter and longer variation of this try adding 3 parts of good-quality pressed apple juice to this recipe and serve in a highball glass.

TYPE: SOURS—ON THE ROCKS   **GLASS:**

- **2 PARTS INFUSED MAPLE SYRUP (GRADE 1 MAPLE SYRUP, VANILLA POD, LARGE CINNAMON STICK)**
- **5 PARTS BOURBON OR TENNESSEE WHISKEY**
- **2.5 PARTS LEMON JUICE**
- **2 DASHES ANGOSTURA BITTERS**
- **1 SMALL EGG WHITE**
- **GARNISH:** CINNAMON STICK, ORANGE TWIST

To make the infused maple syrup, scrape out the seeds from the vanilla pod and add, along with the cinnamon stick, to 8fl oz (225ml) grade 1 maple syrup (this is the lightest in flavor and will not overpower the other ingredients). Leave to infuse for at least 48 hours, then strain. This will keep in the fridge indefinitely and is delicious on pancakes as well.

Shake all ingredients without ice to emulsify the egg white; shake again with ice and then strain all ingredients over fresh ice into a large whiskey glass. Garnish with a cinnamon stick and squeeze the zest of the orange twist over the foam.

↻ Give this a try with brandy instead of American whiskey.

WHISKEY SMASH

The Mint Julep is one of the most famous whiskey cocktails, and almost impossible to make well, especially as you need to swizzle it for ages. The addition of citrus makes balancing this drink easier, shaking it chills it much faster, and the end product is much more refreshing.

TYPE: SOURS—ON THE ROCKS   **GLASS:**

3 LEMON WEDGES
8 MINT LEAVES
5 PARTS BOURBON
2 PARTS SIMPLE SYRUP
GARNISH: SPRIG OF MINT,
   LEMON SLICE

Muddle the lemon wedges and mint in a cocktail shaker, add the other ingredients and shake hard. For a pretty drink strain over cracked ice into a large whiskey glass; for a more rustic one simply pour from the shaker, ice, lemon pieces, and all. Garnish with a lemon slice and a mint sprig that you have gently slapped to release the aroma.

DEVIL'S SHARE

Created by mixologist Pete Kendall and named as a counterpoint to the "angel's share," the spirit that is lost from the barrel through evaporation, this drink is a crisp and zingy variation on a whiskey sour. For those who want it even more spicy, just increase the amount of ginger, or muddle a little into the glass, to infuse as the drink is consumed.

TYPE: SOURS—ON THE ROCKS **GLASS:**

3 SLICES FRESH GINGER

3 LEMON WEDGES

2 ORANGE SLICES

5 PARTS AMERICAN WHISKEY

2 PARTS SIMPLE SYRUP

GARNISH: SLICES OF FRESH
    GINGER, LEMON, AND ORANGE

Muddle the ginger slices, lemon wedges, and orange slices in a cocktail shaker. Add the remaining ingredients and ice and shake hard. Strain over cracked ice into a large whiskey glass and garnish with ginger, lemon, and orange slices.

♻ Rum makes a decent substitute here if you've run out of whiskey.

LOUISIANA JAM

Originally created with Southern Comfort, the apricot preserve in this drink pairs naturally with the soft, sweet Tennessee whiskey. If you fancy making the original, just replace the whiskey with Southern Comfort and omit the simple syrup.

TYPE: SOURS—ON THE ROCKS **GLASS:**

5 PARTS TENNESSEE WHISKEY
2 PARTS APRICOT PRESERVE
2 PARTS LEMON JUICE
I PART SIMPLE SYRUP
8 MINT LEAVES
GARNISH: MINT SPRIGS

Shake all the ingredients with ice and strain over cracked ice into a large whiskey glass. Depending on the level of pectin in the apricot preserve you might want to thin it down a little first with a bit of hot water. For a party, simply put all the ingredients with some cracked ice into a clean preserve jar and let your guests shake their own, then drink straight from the jar.

↻ Brandy will work just as well as the whiskey for this one.

L'N'G

Created by Vincenzo Errico with Woodford Reserve and named for the Labrot + Graham distiller that produces it. However, this drink works well with any American whiskey and is a wonderful drink for those who like a sweeter style of Manhattan.

TYPE: STIRRED—STRAIGHT UP   **GLASS:**

4 PARTS BOURBON
1 PART COINTREAU
1 PART CHAMBORD
GARNISH: 3 RASPBERRIES

Stir the ingredients over ice and strain into a chilled cocktail glass. Garnish with three raspberries speared on a cocktail stick.

HARVEST MOON
PUNCH

Adapted from a recipe by Dale DeGroff, this is an amazing Halloween or bonfire party drink. Dale recommends serving it in a hollowed-out pumpkin—this keeps the drink warm (like a vacuum flask) and looks amazing.

TYPE: HOT DRINKS   GLASS:

2 PARTS BOURBON

3 PARTS PRESSED APPLE JUICE

5 PARTS DRY APPLE CIDER

I PART LEMON JUICE

I PART DEMERARA SIMPLE SYRUP

I CINNAMON STICK

2 CLOVES

I STAR ANISE

I ORANGE ZEST

GARNISH: RED APPLE WEDGE

This drink can be made individually but works even better as a punch to share. Simply multiply the quantities and gently heat all the ingredients in a saucepan for 20 minutes. Do not boil though—you want to keep it below 70°C or all the booze will evaporate. Strain off the spices and serve in a wine goblet.

NEW YORK FLIP

This drink is a fantastic alternative to a dessert—in fact it is almost a dessert and digestif mixed into one! You can use other types of port—tawny, for example—or red wine with a little more simple syrup.

TYPE: FLIPS & AFTER DINNER **GLASS:**

3 PARTS AMERICAN WHISKEY

2 PARTS RUBY PORT

2 PARTS HEAVY (DOUBLE) CREAM

1 PART SIMPLE SYRUP

1 SMALL EGG YOLK

GARNISH: FRESHLY GRATED NUTMEG

Shake all the ingredients very hard with ice for at least 30 seconds. The harder you shake the lighter the texture will be. Strain into a chilled wine glass and grate a little nutmeg over the top.

↻ A tot of brandy instead of the whiskey wouldn't go amiss here.

SCOTCH & IRISH WHISKEY

The three main categories of whisky produced in the UK are blended Scotch, malt Scotch, and Irish whiskey. There are over 900 available whiskies from the British Isles, and to have that kind of diversity over such a small area is amazing.

KEY POINTS TO NOTE

• All whisky is made from grain; in the UK it's all made from one grain in particular—barley. This is the ideal grain as it is easy to germinate and contains a large amount of starch—thereby producing lots of fermentable sugars. There are many factors that affect the taste of the whisky and the most important is the treatment of the raw material. The malting process, where the seeds are fooled into germination, is halted when the sprout first appears. This is done in a variety of ways, and that is where the Scotch and Irish methods differ. Irish whiskeys kiln their malt in a sealed oven while Scotch whiskies use an open fire. Roasting the malt adds a characteristic flavor, which is often compounded by the use of peat as the source of the fire.

• The grain is then soaked and yeast is added. The performance of the yeast is also important to the finished whisky. Samples are cultured and the exact strain will be a closely guarded secret.

• The resulting "beer" is then distilled and for malt whisky this would traditionally be done in copper pot stills, the shape of which determines the style of spirit. Tall, narrow-headed stills produce a lighter whisky, while the short squat still will produce a much meatier and oilier whisky.

• Irish whiskey is normally distilled three times to Scotch's two; grain whisky is generally stilled twice. This further contributes to the smooth, gentle character of Irish whiskeys.

• The distillate is then aged in oak barrels that may have been used many times before. The UK climate dictates a long aging time, and it is the time spent in the barrel that truly differentiates these whiskies from each other—aging conditions vary from distillery to distillery. The salty flavor of Islay whiskies, for example, is down to the constant salty breeze. Some of the most characteristic malts taste more individual than any other spirit.

• The bestselling whiskies are not actually the characterful and individual malts, but blended Scotch whiskies. Brands like Johnnie Walker or Chivas Regal have massive worldwide presence, closely followed by Bell's and Famous Grouse. This style of whisky grew up around the larger cities and towns as merchants strove to produce a consistent whisky from a selection of small amounts of varying styles from different manufacturers. They also took hold of the idea of building a brand—a relatively new thing in the marketing of spirits—and the famous trademarks and names of those blenders on the bottles today suggest that they got it right. Success was due to the fact that the market was rapidly increasing in England as the cognac supply was drying up. The English were not used to the fiery, smoky character of Scotch and so, using the technology of continuous distillation, the producers made blended whiskies based on neutral grain whisky with different proportions of various malts to produce their signature style.

• Scotch malts are classed by various means and it can be difficult to work out the classifications because of the number of styles of production and the proliferation of misfits. However, it is generally accepted that there are five distinct areas (Speyside, Highlands and Islands, Islay, Lowlands, and Campbeltown). There are also four main types of Scotch malt:

1 Single malt is the product of a single distillery and is aged there.

2 Vatted malt is a blend of 100 percent malt whiskies.

3 Blended Scotch is a blend of malts on a grain whisky base.

4 Grain whisky is a continuously distilled neutral spirit with little age.

ROB ROY

Created in 1894 and named after the famous outlaw, often thought of as the Scottish Robin Hood, this drink works well with all styles of blended Scotch whisky and even with some lighter malts. If using a more heavily peated, smoky whisky, you might want to vary the proportions a little in favor of the vermouth.

TYPE: STIRRED—STRAIGHT UP   GLASS:

4 PARTS BLENDED
   SCOTCH WHISKY
2 PARTS SWEET VERMOUTH
2 DASHES ANGOSTURA BITTERS
GARNISH: LEMON OR ORANGE
   TWIST, COCKTAIL CHERRY
   (OPTIONAL)

Stir all the ingredients over ice and strain into a chilled cocktail glass. Squeeze the twist over the surface of the drink to garnish and, if you like them, add a cocktail cherry as well.

AULD LANG SYNE

The Rusty Nail is a great Scotch whisky drink that works well with all styles of blended and malt whisky. I have updated the recipe with a hint of aromatic bitters and a clove-studded lemon. The extra bitterness and hint of citrus cut through the sweetness of the Drambuie to make a cocktail that is easier to drink—having two is even easier.

TYPE: STIRRED—ON THE ROCKS   **GLASS:**

3 PARTS SCOTCH WHISKY
2 PARTS DRAMBUIE
1 DASH ANGOSTURA BITTERS
GARNISH: LEMON SLICE STUDDED WITH CLOVES

Stir all the ingredients over ice and strain into a whisky glass full of fresh ice. Pierce holes in the skin of a lemon slice, insert a few cloves, and add to the glass.

BLOOD AND SAND

One of the first drinks to be created as a film tie-in, in this case the eponymous Rudolph Valentino epic of 1922. This drink is almost one of a kind in its composition, relying on the tartness of blood-orange juice to balance the sweet ingredients. If you can't get hold of blood oranges, regular ones with a squeeze of lemon will suffice. Make sure you use a good-quality cherry liqueur (often wrongly called cherry brandy) that has been made using the stones as well as the fruit. Cherry Heering is an excellent example.

TYPE: SOURS—STRAIGHT UP **GLASS:**

1.5 PARTS BLENDED SCOTCH WHISKY

1.5 PARTS SWEET VERMOUTH

1.5 PARTS CHERRY LIQUEUR

1.5 PARTS BLOOD-ORANGE JUICE

GARNISH: ORANGE TWIST,
COCKTAIL CHERRY

Shake all the ingredients over ice and strain into a chilled cocktail glass. Garnish with the zest from an orange twist and a cherry on a cocktail stick.

THE WEEGIE

Named after the slightly derogatory term for a Glaswegian—particularly one who has visited the Auchentoshan distillery in that fair city—this drink, using some of the ingredients of a Mai Tai, is one of my favorites. The light level of smokiness and peat combines well with the sweet pineapple and almond flavor for a truly tropical whisky drink. If you have the chance you should certainly try this with Auchentoshan Three Wood, one of the best "interesting" whiskies money can buy.

TYPE: COLLINS & HIGHBALLS   **GLASS:**

- 4 PARTS LOWLAND SCOTCH MALT WHISKY
- 2 PARTS COINTREAU
- 2.5 PARTS LEMON JUICE
- 1 PART ORGEAT (ALMOND) SYRUP
- 3 PARTS PINEAPPLE JUICE
- 2 DASHES ANGOSTURA BITTERS
- GARNISH: PINEAPPLE WEDGE AND LEAVES

Shake all the ingredients with ice and strain over ice into a highball glass. Garnish with a wedge of fresh pineapple and, if they look nice, some of the leaves in a fan.

APRICOT
OLD-FASHIONED

Apricot enhances some of the soft fruit flavors found in lighter blends and some lowland malt whiskies. As the ice continues to melt different flavor compounds are released, from both the whisky and the aromatic apricot. This is a lovely introduction to Scotch, as it is wonderfully gentle.

TYPE: STIRRED—ON THE ROCKS   **GLASS:**

I PART APRICOT PRESERVE

2 DASHES REGANS' ORANGE BITTERS

5 PARTS BLENDED SCOTCH WHISKY

GARNISH: LARGE LEMON TWIST

Thin down the apricot preserve with a teaspoon of hot water in a rocks glass, add the bitters and a dash of whisky and stir. Continue to add ice and whisky, while stirring, until the liquid reaches the required level. Garnish with a large lemon twist squeezed onto the surface of the drink.

Brandy goes nicely here with the flavors of apricot and orange.

HONEYED IRISH
OLD-FASHIONED

Irish whiskey is generally triple-distilled and unpeated, so the flavors are much softer than in other whiskeys. This old-fashioned variant tries to keep this delicacy, gently sweetening with honey. You can use any honey but I find for this and most other drinks a light, flowery style works best.

TYPE: STIRRED—ON THE ROCKS **GLASS:**

- 5 PARTS IRISH WHISKEY
- I PART HONEY SYRUP
  (SEE PAGE 36)
- 2 DASHES REGANS'
  ORANGE BITTERS
- GARNISH: LARGE
  LEMON TWIST

Honey syrup is much easier to mix in a cocktail than pure honey, which tends to stick to the glass. Stir all the ingredients over ice and strain over fresh ice into a whiskey glass. Garnish with a well-squeezed lemon twist.

SCOTCH COLLINS

One of the simplest drinks to make and also one of the tastiest—essentially this is just whisky and homemade lemonade. For parties it's easier to make the lemonade in advance in a pitcher and simply pour over ice with the whisky. Give it a quick stir and the party is started.

TYPE: COLLINS & HIGHBALLS   **GLASS:**

5 PARTS BLENDED SCOTCH WHISKY
2.5 PARTS LEMON JUICE
3 PARTS SIMPLE SYRUP
2 DASHES ANGOSTURA BITTERS
7 PARTS SODA WATER
GARNISH: LEMON WEDGE

Stir all the ingredients apart from the soda with ice in a highball glass. Add more ice and fill to the top with soda. Garnish with a large lemon wedge for the drinker to squeeze in if necessary.

↻ Switch up the Scotch whisky and lemon juice for rum and lime juice to enjoy a Rum Collins (see page 80).

PENICILLIN

Created by mixologist Sam Ross, this very approachable Scotch sour is "inoculated" with a hint of heavily peated malt whisky. I recommend Lagavulin, but almost all Islay whiskies will work, as will Talisker. This is a great way to enjoy the aroma of this style of malt, while still having an easy-drinking and refreshing sour.

TYPE: SOURS—ON THE ROCKS   **GLASS:**

- **5 PARTS BLENDED SCOTCH WHISKY**
- **2.5 PARTS LEMON JUICE**
- **2 PARTS GINGER SYRUP (SEE PAGE 73)**
- **1 SMALL EGG WHITE**
- GARNISH: 6 DROPS OF HEAVILY PEATED SMOKY MALT WHISKY

Shake all the ingredients without ice to emulsify the egg white. Shake again with ice and strain over fresh ice into a large whisky glass. Gently drizzle the malt whisky on top of the foam.

There are three options here: switch the blended whisky for tequila, the peated Scotch for mescal, or both.

MARMALADE
SOUR

Although marmalade was initially made in Portugal from quinces, we now associate it with oranges, particularly the bitter oranges from Seville. Scotland, though, has a long association with marmalade, particularly the city of Dundee. It is serendipitous, then, that it mixes so well with Scotch, with the bold orange flavor and pronounced bitterness able to stand up to any blended whisky.

TYPE: SOURS—ON THE ROCKS   **GLASS:**

5 PARTS BLENDED SCOTCH WHISKY

2.5 PARTS LEMON JUICE

1 PART SIMPLE SYRUP

1.5 PARTS SEVILLE ORANGE MARMALADE

1 SMALL EGG WHITE

GARNISH: CURLED ORANGE ZEST STRIPS

This drink tastes fantastic with a splash of bourbon replacing the Scotch.

Shake all the ingredients without ice to emulsify the egg white. Shake again with ice and then strain over fresh ice into a large whisky glass. Garnish with a large orange twist cut into thin strips and curled.

RASPBERRY SOUR

Scotland is justly famed for its raspberries, and for the short time that they are in season a lot of desserts pair them with light, blended whisky for a heavenly marriage. Unfortunately, the berries are pretty flavorless out of season. Using preserve—ideally homemade—gets around this to create a drink to enjoy all year round. If you get hold of good fresh raspberries just use four or five instead of the preserve and add 1 extra part of simple syrup.

TYPE: SOURS—ON THE ROCKS   **GLASS:**

5 PARTS BLENDED SCOTCH WHISKY

2.5 PARTS LEMON JUICE

1 PART SIMPLE SYRUP

1.5 PARTS RASPBERRY PRESERVE

1 SMALL EGG WHITE

GARNISH: LEMON TWIST

Shake all the ingredients without ice to emulsify the egg white, then shake again with ice. Strain over fresh ice into a large whisky glass and garnish with a long, spiraled lemon twist.

WHISKY TODDY

Jerry Thomas, one of the world's most famous bartenders, created a drink called the Blue Blazer, in which water and whisky (in his case bourbon) were poured flaming from glass to glass. He would serve it only when it was cold outside or his patron was ill. His presentation was amazing, but the drink sucked. This is a much more appealing (and effective) toddy to be served as a warmer or pick-me-up. You can use any whisky for this, although my girlfriend swears by Glenmorangie.

TYPE: HOT DRINKS   **GLASS:**

4 PARTS WHISKY

I PART HONEY

I PART LEMON JUICE

8 PARTS BOILING WATER

I DASH ANGOSTURA BITTERS

GARNISH: LONG LEMON TWIST

Mix together all the ingredients in a tempered glass, ideally with a handle (if you are feeling ill a mug works just as well). Squeeze the lemon twist and coil it inside the drink.

IRISH COFFEE

This drink was created at Shannon airport, which used to be a fueling stopover for transatlantic flights. It relies on the counterpoint between hot, sweet, boozy coffee and cold, unsweetened cream. Whipping the cream by hand gives you better control of the texture. Americano coffee (espresso and hot water) will make a more satisfying blend than cafetière coffee, as it is hotter. Anyone using squirty cream from a can should be shot on sight.

TYPE: HOT DRINKS   **GLASS:**

4 PARTS WHIPPING CREAM
2 TSP SUGAR
4 PARTS IRISH WHISKEY
9 PARTS STRONG COFFEE
GARNISH: NONE

Lightly whip the cream until the bubbles on the surface no longer hold. Mix the sugar, whiskey, and coffee together in a heatproof glass or wine goblet. Using a bar spoon, float the cream on the top.

Make this Irish coffee into a French one by using brandy instead of whiskey.

IRISH
APRICOT FLIP

A wonderful after-dinner drink combining the gentle flavors of Irish whiskey, aromatic apricots, and the warmth of honey, delivered on a wave of soft cream. If you have it, you can replace the honey syrup with 1.5 parts of sweet wine—orange muscat works very well.

TYPE: FLIPS & AFTER DINNER **GLASS:**

5 PARTS IRISH WHISKEY

1.5 PARTS APRICOT PRESERVE

1 PART HONEY SYRUP (SEE PAGE 36)

2 PARTS HEAVY (DOUBLE) CREAM

1 SMALL EGG YOLK

GARNISH: ORANGE TWIST

Shake all ingredients very hard with ice for at least 30 seconds. The harder you shake, the lighter the texture will be. Strain into a chilled wine glass and express an orange zest over the foam.

Rum is a good choice here if you want to save your whiskey for a nightcap.

RASPBERRY BLOW FIZZ

This recipe uses tart raspberries to balance the richness of the cream. The egg, properly shaken, will form a magnificent head, making the drink taste like a raspberry whisky cloud. Divine.

TYPE: FLIPS & AFTER DINNER   GLASS:

5 PARTS BLENDED SCOTCH WHISKY
2 PARTS HEAVY (DOUBLE) CREAM
2.5 PARTS SIMPLE SYRUP
6 RASPBERRIES
I SMALL EGG
2 PARTS SODA WATER
GARNISH: NONE

Shake all the ingredients apart from the soda water very hard for at least 40 seconds. Strain into a chilled highball glass and slowly add soda water until the foam rises above the rim of the glass.

SCOTCH & GINGER

This is one of the great simple drinks and perfect for the summer. I have spiced it up with the addition of some homemade ginger syrup to bring an extra kick, working well with even the heaviest blended whiskies.

TYPE: COLLINS & HIGHBALLS   GLASS:

I PART GINGER SYRUP (FRESH GINGER, SUPERFINE (CASTER) SUGAR)
5 PARTS BLENDED SCOTCH WHISKY
IO PARTS GINGER ALE
GARNISH: LEMON WEDGE

To make the syrup, blend fresh ginger in a food processor or juice extractor and mix the resultant juice with the same weight of superfine (caster) sugar. This syrup will last a couple of weeks in the refrigerator in an airtight jar. Pour the ingredients over ice into a highball glass and briefly stir. Garnish with a squeezed lemon wedge.

RUM

Rum is defined as a spirit made from sugar cane or its residues and, as such, the term covers the broadest spectrum of flavors and styles of any spirit. The word rum is probably derived from either the Latin name for sugar cane, *saccharum*, or the old English word *rumbullion*, which means roughly the same thing.

KEY POINTS TO NOTE

• Rum can be easily split into two groups, depending on the raw materials used in its production. The English styles of rum, made all over the world but originally in the British islands of the Caribbean, use molasses, the by-product of sugar manufacturing, as the base, while the French rhum agricole uses the juice of unprocessed sugar cane. Each group has a variety of styles, but this is the most basic difference.

• The rum of Brazil, Cachaca, is a rhum agricole with a slight difference: the fibrous material from the sugar cane is included in its distillation. This is what gives Cachaca its definitive vegetal flavor.

• The English style of rum is far more common, probably owing not only to its accessibility but also to the fact that the English Navy was much more active in the trade in slaves and sugar and so would have taken their style with them as they sailed around the world. Rhum agricole is, in most cases, produced in much smaller quantities, and its distribution is less widespread.

• Within the English rum category there are differences in style, which come down to local production methods and climate, but most of the changes happen after the rum is distilled. Rum can be further split into the categories light, golden, and dark.

• Light rums are almost always aged and then filtered back to clarity with charcoal. These are the most common style and the one that works best in the clean, citrus-based drinks of Cuba. Good white rum should have a clean and neutral nose with a hint of sweetness on the palate.

• Golden rums are produced by either aging white rum in oak barrels, similar to other spirits, or by adding caramel or other sugars to give color and body. Golden rums that have been aged are far superior in flavor and are the most versatile of all the rums.

• With dark rums you see the split between aging and coloring more clearly. Navy rums like Lambs, Myers, and Woods 100 are all unaged products with the addition of flavorsome sugars; the deep black color and smell are both suggestive of molasses. These rums are very traditional and almost vital for the making of good punch-style cocktails—their strong flavor will carry over the likes of orgeat and pineapple juice. The other dark rums are the long-aged boutique rums produced by many distilleries. These are some of the finest examples of any bottled spirit. In the Caribbean, aging takes place at an accelerated rate. You would expect the oldest rums to be little more than wood water, but something in the character of the slightly sweet rum allows the wood to integrate, producing great tobacco, leather, and chocolate flavors—the equal of almost any cognac.

•The French-style manufacturers also produce aged products (although no colored rums at a premium level). Indeed, some of the finest rums in the world are the old Martinique rums.

RUM MANHATTAN

Rum is such a varied category, with each distiller, island, and country producing many different styles. Almost all aged rums will make great Manhattan variations, but the sweet spot is probably with rums around 7–8 years old, where they have taken on character from their aging but also retain some sweet, young rum characteristics.

TYPE: STIRRED—STRAIGHT UP **GLASS:**

4 PARTS RUM
2 PARTS SWEET VERMOUTH
2 DASHES ANGOSTURA BITTERS
GARNISH: LARGE ORANGE TWIST

Stir all the ingredients over ice and strain into a chilled cocktail glass. Squeeze the orange twist over the surface of the drink and add as a garnish.

RUM
OLD-FASHIONED

Rum has a natural affinity with its raw material—sugar—but as some have a residual sweetness it is always worth experimenting with the amount. Start with just half a cube—you can always add more but you can't take any away. You can also play around with the type of sugar; with demerara, muscovado, or even a hint of treacle making fantastic Rum Old-Fashioneds.

TYPE: STIRRED—ON THE ROCKS   **GLASS:**

I CUBE BROWN SUGAR

5 PARTS RUM

2 DASHES ANGOSTURA BITTERS

GARNISH: LIME AND ORANGE
ZESTS, CINNAMON STICK

Crush the sugar cube in a tumbler with a dash of the rum and the bitters. Add ice and the remaining rum a little at a time, stirring continuously with a cinnamon stick until the liquid reaches the required level. Thoroughly squeeze the oils from the lime and orange twists and add to the drink. Serve with the cinnamon stick as a stirrer.

CUBANADA

Soft, sweet maple works very well with good golden rum, particularly those with pronounced oak flavors and full-bodied English Island rums like ones from Jamaica. If using a lighter-bodied rum, consider cutting the maple syrup down to 1 part and adding the equivalent amount of simple syrup.

TYPE: SOURS—STRAIGHT UP   **GLASS**:

5 PARTS RUM
2 PARTS MAPLE SYRUP
2 PARTS LIME JUICE
2 DASHES ANGOSTURA BITTERS
GARNISH: LIME WHEEL

Shake all the ingredients with ice and fine-strain into a chilled cocktail glass. Garnish with a thin lime wheel on the rim of the glass.

♺ Swap your limes for lemons and your rum for bourbon, add an egg white, and you've got a St Lawrence (see page 51).

AMBROSIA

Ambrosia was the nectar of the gods, and this drink comes pretty close to recreating it. The rums of Cuba have a character all their own, mostly because they are aged in old oak casks that have been filled many times. Their dry, tannic flavors are softened by the honey to make a complex but easy-drinking recipe.

TYPE: SOURS—STRAIGHT UP **GLASS:**

5 PARTS CUBAN RUM

2 PARTS HONEY SYRUP
   (SEE PAGE 36)

2 PARTS LIME JUICE

2 DASHES ANGOSTURA
   BITTERS

GARNISH: ORANGE TWIST

Shake all the ingredients with ice and fine-strain into a chilled cocktail glass. Squeeze the zest from the orange twist over the surface of the drink and add to the glass as a garnish.

RUM COLLINS

This simple and refreshing drink is great for showing off the characteristics of different rums and works equally well with light, golden, and dark rums. It also makes a great drink to share: simply up the quantities and serve in a chilled pitcher with glasses and lots of ice. Serve—ideally—by the pool.

TYPE: COLLINS & HIGHBALLS **GLASS:**

5 PARTS RUM
3 PARTS SIMPLE SYRUP
2.5 PARTS LIME JUICE
6 PARTS SODA WATER
3 DASHES ANGOSTURA BITTERS
GARNISH: LIME WEDGE

Pour the first three ingredients over ice into a highball glass. Top with soda water and then add the Angostura bitters. Garnish with a lime wedge on the rim.

MOJITO

This is one of the world's most popular cocktails, and there are enough different recipes and methods of making it to fill a book on their own. This one is the easiest and most consistent of them all. When making the drink, muddle the mint only lightly; it doesn't take a lot to release the aroma. If making crushed ice is too much hassle for you, a great version can be made using cubed ice and soda water to top up.

TYPE: COLLINS & HIGHBALLS   **GLASS:**

8 MINT LEAVES
5 PARTS CUBAN RUM
2 PARTS LIME JUICE
2 PARTS SIMPLE SYRUP
GARNISH: MINT SPRIG

Gently muddle the mint in a large highball glass. Add the other ingredients and swizzle with crushed ice. Garnish with a mint sprig.

DAIQUIRI

Originally created with white rum, this works well with any rum. Most white rums are aged and then filtered back to clarity anyway. Cuban and Cuban-style rums work particularly well, their almost medicinal and grassy notes complementing the crisp, fresh lime. Some people like their daiquiris quite sour so I always add a lime wedge that can be squeezed in. When trying a new rum, experiment with the sugar levels to balance the particular spirit.

TYPE: SOURS—STRAIGHT UP   **GLASS:**

5 PARTS RUM
2 PARTS LIME JUICE
1.5–2 PARTS SIMPLE SYRUP
GARNISH: LIME WEDGE

Shake all the ingredients with ice and fine-strain into a chilled cocktail glass. Garnish with a lime wedge on the rim to allow the drinker to make the drink more tart, if required.

STRAWBERRY
DAIQUIRI

The Strawberry Daiquiri has—unfairly—a bad reputation, owing to the proliferation of terrible frozen versions made with artificial strawberry flavoring and powdered sour mix. This recipe is totally different, with a wonderful balance between rum and soft fruit. If you fancy, you can replace the strawberries with six fresh raspberries and a splash more simple syrup for an equally tasty Raspberry Daiquiri.

TYPE: SOURS—STRAIGHT UP   **GLASS:**

2 STRAWBERRIES
5 PARTS RUM
2 PARTS LIME JUICE
2 PARTS SIMPLE SYRUP
GARNISH: STRAWBERRY
   SLICED INTO A FAN

Muddle the strawberries in a Boston shaker, add the other ingredients, and shake with ice. Fine-strain into a chilled cocktail glass and garnish with a strawberry fan.

DRY DAIQUIRI

Created by superstar bartender Kevin Armstrong, this excellent recipe brings both floral notes and a pleasing bitterness to a classic Daiquiri—perfect as an aperitif in the summer. Campari lovers may want to up the quantity a little; just remember that as it is quite sweet, the simple syrup may need to be reined in a little.

TYPE: SOURS—STRAIGHT UP   **GLASS:**

4.5 PARTS RUM

1.5 PARTS SIMPLE SYRUP

2 PARTS LIME JUICE

0.5 PART CAMPARI

1 DASH PASSION-FRUIT SYRUP

GARNISH: ORANGE TWIST

Shake all the ingredients with ice and fine-strain into a chilled cocktail glass. Squeeze the zest from the orange twist over the surface of the drink and add to the glass to garnish.

CUBA LIBRE

I would never normally consider putting a cola-based drink in a cocktail book, but if you make a Cuba Libre with Havana 7 Year Old or similar it tastes so fantastic! It's easy to make—just be sure to keep the Coca-Cola in the refrigerator, and if possible buy the glass-bottled version, as it tastes better than those in plastic or from a can. This is a great drink to serve to your unreconstructed friends who may be a bit "sniffy" about cocktails; once they have had your Cuba Libre they will be more willing to be adventurous.

TYPE: COLLINS & HIGHBALLS   **GLASS:**

5 PARTS CUBAN RUM

1.5 PARTS LIME JUICE

9 PARTS COCA-COLA

GARNISH: LIME WEDGES

Build all the ingredients over cubed ice in a highball glass and garnish with two lime wedges.

SHELTER FROM
THE STORM

The original Dark'n'Stormy is one of the few trademarked cocktails, and should be made with Goslings Black Seal rum. This variation adds orange notes from the Curaçao and almond from the orgeat syrup, and can be made with any aged or dark rum. Make sure you get a nice spicy ginger beer; if necessary, a couple of thin slices of fresh ginger can be stirred in to bolster the flavor.

TYPE: COLLINS & HIGHBALLS   GLASS:

4 PARTS AGED OR DARK RUM

I PART ORANGE CURAÇAO OR COINTREAU

I PART ORGEAT (ALMOND) SYRUP

2 PARTS LIME JUICE

8 PARTS GOOD-QUALITY GINGER BEER

GARNISH: GINGER SLICE (OPTIONAL), LIME WEDGE

Add the first four ingredients to a large highball filled with cubed ice and stir. Top up with the ginger beer and garnish with a slice of ginger and a lime wedge.

ANEJO HIGHBALL

Created by Dale DeGroff, this drink uses the "Holy Trinity" of the Caribbean—rum, lime, and Curaçao—and makes a Douglas Adams–style trinity in five parts with the addition of two more typical island flavors: ginger and aromatic bitters. The drink works best with an aged Cuban rum, but feel free to try it with any rum. It is a remarkably forgiving and adaptable recipe.

TYPE: COLLINS & HIGHBALLS   **GLASS:**

4 PARTS CUBAN RUM

2 PARTS ORANGE CURAÇAO

2 PARTS LIME JUICE

2 DASHES ANGOSTURA BITTERS

8 PARTS GINGER BEER

GARNISH: LIME WHEEL, ORANGE SLICE

Add the first four ingredients to a highball glass filled with ice. Stir well, top up with ginger beer and garnish with a lime wheel and orange slice.

Some bourbon or Tennessee whiskey would work just as well as the rum in this cocktail.

MAI TAI

The original Mai Tai was created either by Don the Beachcomber or Trader Vic—two legendary Tiki bar owners—and named for the Tahitian expression for "very good" or "out of this world." Due to the conflicting stories and recipes, this is my own version, which I think is better than both. If you can find an overproof dark rum, it will float much more easily and also give the drink a real kick.

TYPE: SOURS—ON THE ROCKS **GLASS:**

4 PARTS GOLD RUM

2 PARTS ORANGE CURAÇAO

I PART ORGEAT (ALMOND) SYRUP

2 PARTS LIME JUICE

I DASH ANGOSTURA BITTERS

I PART DARK RUM

GARNISH: LIME WEDGE, MINT SPRIG, COCKTAIL CHERRY

Shake the first five ingredients with ice and strain into a large rocks glass over cubed ice. Gently float the dark rum over the surface and then garnish with the lime wedge, mint sprig, and cherry.

CARIBBEAN
FLIP

This warming, spiced after-dinner drink is rich and luxurious and not a little boozy. Any rum can be used to give very different flavor profiles—dark rums produce deep, rich notes of spice and brown sugar, while lighter rums bring out orange notes and the aromatics from the bitters. If you are feeling very brave, a little dash of stout in the recipe is a wonderful thing.

TYPE: FLIPS & AFTER DINNER   **GLASS:**

4 PARTS RUM

I PART ORANGE CURAÇAO

2 PARTS DEMERARA SYRUP

3 PARTS HEAVY (DOUBLE) CREAM

2 DASHES ANGOSTURA BITTERS

I PINCH OF GROUND CINNAMON

I SMALL EGG YOLK

GARNISH: CINNAMON STICK, FRESHLY GRATED NUTMEG

Shake all the ingredients very hard with ice for at least 30 seconds; the harder you shake, the lighter the texture will be. Strain into a chilled wine glass and garnish with a long stick of cinnamon and some freshly grated nutmeg.

If you like this one, why not experiment by using brandy in place of the rum.

SPICED CARIBBEAN
TODDY

Although there isn't much call for hot cocktails in the Caribbean, in colder climes we can appreciate the warm character of rum in a toddy. This recipe is great for when the sun goes down on a clear night and the temperature falls before the party is over. You won't feel the cold after a couple of these.

TYPE: HOT DRINKS   **GLASS:**

3 PARTS RUM

2 PARTS ORANGE CURAÇAO

1 PART LEMON JUICE

3 PARTS ORANGE JUICE

2 PARTS DEMERARA SYRUP

2 DASHES ANGOSTURA BITTERS

1 CINNAMON STICK

2 CLOVES

GARNISH: ORANGE TWIST,
CINNAMON STICK

Heat all the ingredients apart from the rum in a saucepan over a low heat. Just before it comes to the boil, remove it from the heat, add the rum, and stir. Strain into a goblet or Irish coffee glass and garnish with an orange twist and a cinnamon stick.

RUM SOMBRERO

Tia Maria is a rum-based coffee liqueur, which works very well in this drink. You can, of course, use other coffee liqueurs, but just remember that Tia Maria is less sweet than most so you may want to omit the demerara syrup. This drink also works well without the espresso; simply stir the ingredients with ice, strain, and float the cream.

TYPE: FLIPS & AFTER DINNER   **GLASS:**

- 4 PARTS RUM
- 2 PARTS TIA MARIA
- I PART ESPRESSO
- I DASH DEMERARA SYRUP
- 2 PARTS HEAVY (DOUBLE) CREAM, LIGHTLY WHIPPED

GARNISH: COFFEE BEANS OR PINCH OF GROUND CINNAMON

Shake the first four ingredients with ice and strain into a chilled cocktail glass. Float the lightly whipped cream on top and garnish with three coffee beans or a pinch of ground cinnamon.

It's not the most well-known combination, but tequila will work really well with the coffee here.

BRANDY

Brandy is defined as a spirit made from the distillation of fruit-based products, not grain. The most common type of brandy is made from grapes, but there are prominent examples of brandies made from fruit of many sorts, from cherries to plums, apples, pears, and raspberries.

KEY POINTS TO NOTE

• To make brandy you first need to ferment the fruit, in the same way as you would a grain product. Stone fruits, such as peaches and cherries, can be distilled as they are, but raspberries and other soft fruit need the addition of sugars to begin the fermentation. The result is distilled in a variety of ways to form a fruit eau de vie. In the case of soft fruits this is normally drunk unaged and is a heady combination of fruit and alcoholic notes. Some of these brandies are aged, the most notable being Calvados, made from apples in Normandy, France. Calvados responds well to aging.

• By far the majority of brandies are made from grapes. In fact, the word brandy is derived from the Dutch for "burnt wine," although the ideal qualities for good brandy aren't necessarily the same as those for great wine.

• By far the most famous brandies in the world are those that take their name from the small town in northwest France where they are made. Cognac and the surrounding areas of the Charente and Charente Maritime have been producing fine brandies for hundreds of years, and although the method of production is fairly standard, brandies from this area demonstrate the process perfectly.

• Cognac is made primarily from the Ugni Blanc grape with some Colombard or Folle Blanche. These grapes produce a low-strength acidic wine, the very characteristics that stand up best to distillation.

- The area is classified into six growing areas: Grand Champagne, Petit Champagne, Borderies, Fin Bois, Bon Bois, and Bois Ordinaires, ranked in that order. The grapes from these regions are influenced by soil conditions, and the two Champagne regions are reckoned to produce a spirit that, although it takes longer to mature, will make a more complex product.

- These ratings are often alluded to on a bottle of cognac; fine champagne cognac means that the cognac contains only eau de vie from these two areas in its blend, with at least 50 percent coming from the Grande Champagne region.

- The most obvious classification is based on statements of age. V.S. or Very Special is a minimum of two and a half years old, while V.S.O.P. or Very Special Old Pale is at least four years old and X.O. at least six years old. In practice, these minimum ages are not approached in any but the most basic blends. They are mostly there to appeal to different target markets—the Cognac houses have been producing a luxury product for many years now and know exactly what they are doing.

- The spirits produced by the Cognac houses are all blends containing between 15 and 100 different cru from varying vineyards and vintages. The master blender then creates a blend that matches the house's particular style.

- The eau de vie is aged in wood for up to 50 years, after which it is transferred to glass demi-johns, which keep the brandy from deteriorating. Many Cognac houses will still have eau de vie from the 1700s and 1800s.

- The other great French brandy is Armagnac, produced in Gascony in southwest France. It is distilled only once in its own unique still, called an alambic, and the hotter temperature and simple distillation produce a spirit far more earthy than cognac but still of a very high quality. The three regions of Armagnac have similar ratings: Bas, Haut, and Ténarèze, with Bas being the most sought after. Armagnac also differs from cognac in that it is regularly released as a vintage spirit, the produce of just one year.

- Other grape brandies are made around the world, but the one you are most likely to come across in cocktails is Pisco. This brandy is produced in Chile and Peru from Muscat grapes. It is usually unaged, but the use of sweet grapes gives it a flavor with more than a hint of sweetness.

HARVARD

Created in 1895, this cousin of the Manhattan is almost unique among drinks of its type, owing to the addition of soda water. The combination of two grape-based liquors can be almost too seamless; the soda lightens the mixture and really brings out the aromatics from the cognac. Feel free to omit it for a decadent and rich concoction.

TYPE: STIRRED—STRAIGHT UP **GLASS:**

3.5 PARTS COGNAC
1.5 PARTS SWEET VERMOUTH
2 DASHES ANGOSTURA BITTERS
1.5 PARTS SODA WATER
GARNISH: LARGE ORANGE TWIST

Stir all the ingredients apart from the soda water with ice and strain into a chilled cocktail glass. Gently add the soda water, squeeze the oil from a large orange twist, and drape over the rim of the glass.

BRANDY
OLD-FASHIONED

This drink works very well with cognac, Armagnac, Spanish, and Greek brandies (or indeed aged brandies from anywhere else—feel free to try it with Calvados or a good cider brandy). Fine cognacs tend to have a little more sweetness than your average whiskey, so I serve this with a spoon, deliberately leaving some of the sugar undissolved. The drinker can then mix it up to their preference.

TYPE: STIRRED—ON THE ROCKS   **GLASS:**

I CUBE BROWN SUGAR
2 DASHES ANGOSTURA BITTERS
5 PARTS AGED BRANDY
GARNISH: LARGE ORANGE
  TWIST

Gently crush the sugar with the bitters and a little of your chosen brandy in a whiskey glass. Continue adding brandy and ice, stirring all the time, until the liquid reaches the required level. Squeeze a large orange twist over the surface of the drink to release the oils and serve with the twist and a spoon.

APPLE SOUR

A great autumnal sour, using the malic acid in the apple juice to bring a lovely, crisp bite. Any good apple brandy will work well with this recipe, with some young Somerset cider brandies making a particularly refreshing version.

TYPE: SOURS—ON THE ROCKS **GLASS:**

5 PARTS CALVADOS OR OTHER APPLE
  BRANDY
2 PARTS LEMON JUICE
2 PARTS FRESH APPLE JUICE
2 PARTS SIMPLE SYRUP
1 SMALL EGG WHITE
GARNISH: APPLE CHEVRON

First shake all the ingredients without ice to emulsify the egg white. Shake again with ice and then strain over fresh ice into a large whiskey glass. To make an apple chevron, take half an apple and cut a wedge in it, leaving it in place. Cut a smaller wedge within the first and repeat a couple more times. Gently slide out the wedges to create the chevron shape.

B & B SOUR

Bénédictine is a herbaceous, honey-sweetened liqueur. Brandy and Bénédictine are classic bedfellows; indeed the manufacturer even makes a pre-mixed blend. This sour uses this synchronicity to its advantage, with the herbal notes working brilliantly with the cognac, and the honey balancing the tartness of the lemon.

TYPE: SOURS—ON THE ROCKS   **GLASS:**

3 PARTS COGNAC
2 PARTS BÉNÉDICTINE
2 PARTS LEMON JUICE
0.5 PARTS SIMPLE SYRUP
2 DASHES ANGOSTURA BITTERS
1 SMALL EGG WHITE
GARNISH: LARGE ORANGE TWIST

First shake all the ingredients without ice to emulsify the egg white. Shake again with ice and strain over fresh ice into a large whiskey glass. Squeeze the orange twist thoroughly over the surface of the drink and add to the glass to garnish.

PISCO SOUR

Pisco is the national spirit of both Chile and Peru, a brandy made from the Muscat grape. Unaged Pisco is the most commonly found and makes a great sour, but if you can find an aged one the drink develops an extra level of complexity. Either way, this is a fantastic summer drink, aperitif, or even a drink to serve at dinner.

TYPE: SOURS—ON THE ROCKS   GLASS:

5 PARTS PISCO
2.5 PARTS LEMON JUICE
2 PARTS SIMPLE SYRUP
I SMALL EGG WHITE
GARNISH: 6 DROPS
   ANGOSTURA BITTERS

First shake all the ingredients without ice to emulsify the egg white. Shake again with ice and then strain into a wine goblet. Carefully drop the bitters through the foam to garnish; they should slowly bleed into the drink.

APPLEJACK RABBIT

Created by Dale DeGroff, this cocktail is a great session drink or digestif. The warm, rich flavor of the maple syrup complements the fresh citrus and apple notes from the juice and the brandy. Please feel free to adjust the level of maple syrup to your preference, as some are very sweet.

TYPE: SOURS—STRAIGHT UP **GLASS:**

4 PARTS APPLEJACK OR CALVADOS

2 PARTS LEMON JUICE

2 PARTS ORANGE JUICE

2 PARTS MAPLE SYRUP

GARNISH: CINNAMON SUGAR RIM

Shake all the ingredients with ice and strain into a chilled cocktail glass that has been first rimmed with a mixture of 1 part ground cinnamon and 3 parts superfine (caster) sugar. Simply wet the rim of the glass slightly and dip into the sugar. The remaining cinnamon sugar will keep indefinitely.

↻ The orange and lime flavors of this cocktail would work perfectly with a good bourbon.

BRANDY SOUR

This cocktail can be made with any brandy, and is therefore a great catch-all recipe. Most young brandies have notes of green apple in the aroma; if your apple juice is really tasty try it with Calvados or Applejack for a wonderful apple medley.

TYPE: SOURS—STRAIGHT UP   **GLASS:**

5 PARTS BRANDY

2 PARTS LEMON JUICE

2 PARTS PRESSED APPLE JUICE

2 PARTS SIMPLE SYRUP

GARNISH: APPLE FAN DUSTED WITH CINNAMON

Shake all the ingredients with ice and strain into a chilled cocktail glass. To garnish, arrange thin apple slices into a fan shape and lightly dust with cinnamon. Spread the slices out slightly and place on the rim of the glass.

BIG APPLEBERRY

The key to the very best fruit drinks is pretty obvious—use good fruit. This recipe works well with pretty much any red fruits, so use whatever is currently good and in season: raspberries, strawberries, redcurrants, and blackberries are all fantastic partners to brandy. The red grapes provide a little extra sweetness but can be omitted—just add a dash more simple syrup.

TYPE: COLLINS & HIGHBALLS   **GLASS:**

I BLACKBERRY

5 RASPBERRIES

3 RED GRAPES

I STRING REDCURRANTS

5 PARTS COGNAC

I PART SIMPLE SYRUP

6 PARTS APPLE JUICE

GARNISH: REDCURRANTS AND
   RASPBERRIES

Muddle the fruits lightly, add all the other ingredients and shake with ice. Strain into a large highball glass and garnish with raspberries and redcurrants.

CALIFORNIA SOUL

A great summer drink, this white sangria can easily be made in a punch bowl for a picnic or barbecue. Chardonnay works really well with honey and pink grapefruit, but any white wine that is not too acidic will be good. If you are making up a large batch for a party, make it in advance and leave to chill in the refrigerator so that the wonderful aromas from the fresh fruit infuse into the drink.

TYPE: COLLINS & HIGHBALLS **GLASS:**

3 PARTS COGNAC

I PART LEMON JUICE

I PART HONEY SYRUP (SEE PAGE 36)

2 ORANGE SLICES

4 PINK GRAPEFRUIT SLICES

5 PARTS CHARDONNAY

GARNISH: SLICES OF FRUIT,
   MINT SPRIG

Pour all the ingredients over ice into a large highball glass and stir to release some of the juice from the orange and grapefruit slices. Add lots more fruit to garnish and top with a fresh mint sprig.

SANGRIA

There are hundreds of recipes for sangria; this is one of the simplest, but if you use good ingredients it can also be one of the best. I like a full-bodied wine, but not one that has spent too much time in the barrel. If you are looking to make a traditional sangria, a young Rioja or other Tempranillo-based wine is fantastic.

TYPE: COLLINS & HIGHBALLS   **GLASS:**

2 PARTS COGNAC
I PART LEMON JUICE
I PART SIMPLE SYRUP
3 ORANGE SLICES
6 PARTS RED WINE
GARNISH: ORANGE AND
    LEMON SLICES

Pour all the ingredients over ice into a large wine goblet and stir. Garnish with orange and lemon slices.

It might not please the traditionalists, but swapping the cognac for bourbon makes a delicious beverage.

SIDECAR

Created around the end of World War One, this is the archetypal straight-up brandy sour. The recipe below makes a slightly sour drink, mitigated by the sugar rim, so feel free to up the measure of Cointreau or even add a dash of simple syrup to make a slightly sweeter version.

TYPE: SOURS—STRAIGHT UP   **GLASS**:

4 PARTS COGNAC
2 PARTS COINTREAU
2 PARTS LEMON JUICE
GARNISH: SUGAR RIM (LEMON JUICE AND SUPERFINE/CASTER SUGAR)

Shake all the ingredients with ice and strain into a chilled glass that you have pre-garnished with a sugar rim. Simply wet the rim of the glass slightly with lemon juice and dip into superfine (caster) sugar. For a neater effect try sprinkling the sugar from above—the glasses can then be chilled in the normal way.

CYDER CAR

This is one of my all-time favorite cocktails—strong, long, and refreshing. Most dry ciders will work well, but if you can find a vintage cider that has spent a little time in oak, the extra complexity marries very well with the cognac. Henry Westons Vintage is my recommendation, but be warned, it is 8.2% ABV.

TYPE: COLLINS & HIGHBALLS   **GLASS:**

3 PARTS COGNAC

5 PARTS PRESSED APPLE JUICE

1.5 PARTS COINTREAU

1.5 PARTS LEMON JUICE

6 PARTS STRONG CIDER

GARNISH: LEMON AND APPLE WEDGES

Shake all the ingredients with ice apart from the cider and strain into a large highball or tankard. Top with the cider and add wedges of lemon and apple to garnish.

RASPBERRY FLIP

Technically this is not a flip as it uses the egg white as well as the yolk, but I think the delicate flavors of the raspberries benefit from the even more frothy texture that egg white brings. If raspberries aren't in season, this drink can be made with a tablespoon of good-quality raspberry preserve; just reduce the amount of simple syrup to 1.5 parts.

TYPE: FLIPS & AFTER DINNER   **GLASS:**

5 PARTS COGNAC
2 PARTS HEAVY (DOUBLE) CREAM
3 PARTS SIMPLE SYRUP
1 SMALL EGG
6 RASPBERRIES
GARNISH: 3 RASPBERRIES

Shake all the ingredients very hard with ice for at least 30 seconds; the harder you shake, the lighter the texture will be. Strain into a chilled wine glass and garnish with three fresh raspberries placed gently on the froth.

CHOCOLATE FLIP

The Brandy Alexander is probably the most famous brandy cocktail; to make it just omit the egg yolk from this recipe and garnish with freshly grated nutmeg. I think this version is better and provides a great alternative to a dessert.

TYPE: FLIPS & AFTER DINNER   **GLASS:**

4 PARTS COGNAC
2 PARTS CHOCOLATE LIQUEUR
2 PARTS HEAVY (DOUBLE) CREAM
1 PART SIMPLE SYRUP
1 SMALL EGG YOLK
GARNISH: DARK CHOCOLATE SHARD

Shake all the ingredients very hard with ice for at least 30 seconds; the harder you shake, the lighter the texture will be. Strain into a chilled wine glass and garnish with a piece of good-quality dark chocolate.

↻ A really versatile recipe this one; the cognac can be switched for either rum or any US whiskey.

BLACK CHERRY
ALEXANDER

Chocolate and black cherries go really well together; here the addition of
a cherry syrup to a standard Brandy Alexander tastes fantastic. Luxardo
produce very good cherries in syrup, which are perfect for this recipe;
do not use maraschino cherries, though, as the flavor is very artificial.

TYPE: FLIPS & AFTER DINNER   **GLASS:**

4 PARTS COGNAC

I PART CHOCOLATE LIQUEUR

I PART CHERRY SYRUP

2 PARTS HEAVY (DOUBLE) CREAM

GARNISH: CHOCOLATE
SHAVINGS

Shake all the ingredients hard and strain
into a chilled cocktail glass. Shave some
good-quality chocolate over the surface
of the drink to garnish.

PORT & BRANDY

A very old combination, pre-dating the creation of the cocktail, and often served without ice. I think port can sometimes be a bit cloying, so the extra water from stirring and the ice can help mollify this. I recommend using a Late Bottled Vintage (LBV) port for this, although some good ruby ports also work well.

TYPE: STIRRED—ON THE ROCKS   **GLASS:**

3 PARTS AGED BRANDY
2 PARTS LBV PORT
GARNISH: LEMON TWIST

Stir the ingredients over ice and strain over fresh ice into a whisky tumbler or sturdy brandy balloon. Garnish with a large lemon twist.

TEQUILA & MESCAL

Tequila is the national spirit of Mexico and one of the most individual spirits on the planet. It is also surrounded with many myths and half-truths.

KEY POINTS TO NOTE

• Tequila is the product of the blue agave (*Agave tequilana Weber*). A large relative of the lily (not a cactus), the plant is a leaf succulent and looks very much like the top of a pineapple.

• The agave takes between 8 and 12 years to mature, which means it is difficult for the industry to cope with fluctuations in demand. The plants are supervised: as they reach maturity they produce a large, spiky flower head, which is removed by the harvester. This concentrates the starch in the bulky heart.

• When the plant is ready for harvest, the spiky leaves are cut off and the large heart, which can be far in excess of 220lb (100kg), is transported to the distillery. It is then steamed and fermented to produce pulque—a kind of agave beer. This is then distilled.

• Tequila is subject to government-based classification; every distillery must have a Norma Oficial de Mexico (NOM) number, which will be printed on the bottle.

• Tequila is usually twice-distilled, but there are some exceptions. Regardless, all tequilas come off the still at a low proof, ensuring a full range of agave characters in the final spirit.

• The first classification of tequila is between mixto and 100 percent blue agave. Mixto tequilas can have up to 49 percent sugar from other sources used in its production. These tequilas are never as good as the 100 percent real thing. After this tequila is split into five categories:

1 Blanco or Silver, aged less than 60 days in metal or wood.

2 Joven Abocado, with added caramel but unaged—the "gold" tequila.

3 Reposado, aged in wood between 61 days and one year.

4 Anejo, aged for more than one year.

5 Extra Anejo, aged in wood for more than three years.

• The climate in Mexico ensures very rapid aging, with few tequilas being aged for even five years. Producers want to retain some of the character of the agave, and the wood quickly overpowers it.

• In addition to these stipulations, tequila is also categorized by area of production; only five areas in Mexico can produce tequila.

• A product made from other agave species or outside these areas is known as Mescal. The differences in flavor can be made more pronounced by roasting the heart over wood fires, lending a characteristic smoky note to the spirit.

• The worm in Mescal is actually one of two types of moth larvae that live in the cactus. They were originally used to show proof of the alcoholic level in the container.

TEQUILA
MANHATTAN

The incredible aromatics of both agave and oak that characterize Anejo tequila make a wonderful version of the Manhattan, blending subtly with the herbaceous notes of the vermouth and bitters to produce a truly heady aroma and character. You can use Extra Anejo tequilas in this recipe, but some of the wonderfully vibrant citrus and herbal notes will be lost.

TYPE: STIRRED—STRAIGHT UP   **GLASS:**

4 PARTS ANEJO TEQUILA
2 PARTS SWEET VERMOUTH
2 DASHES ANGOSTURA BITTERS
GARNISH: LEMON TWIST,
  COCKTAIL CHERRY

Stir the ingredients over ice and strain into a chilled cocktail glass. Squeeze the orange twist over the surface of the drink to express the oil and then garnish with the twist and a cocktail cherry.

TEQUILA
OLD-FASHIONED

Good-quality tequila needs very little to bring out its fantastic flavor. Unlike with most of the other old-fashioneds in the book, I have not specified Angostura bitters (although they work very well), as this drink benefits from a lighter style of bitters, especially when using a Reposado tequila—orange bitters work particularly well. If you can find it, the original packaged bitters, Peychaud's, adds a wonderful anise note to this sublime drink.

TYPE: STIRRED—ON THE ROCKS   **GLASS:**

- 1 SUGAR CUBE
- 5 PARTS REPOSADO OR ANEJO TEQUILA
- 2 DASHES AROMATIC BITTERS
- GARNISH: LONG LIME TWIST

Crush the sugar cube in a dash of the tequila and bitters in a tumbler. Add ice and tequila a little bit at a time, stirring all the time, until the liquid reaches the required level. Thoroughly squeeze the oils from the lime twist and add to the drink. Serve with a stirrer or spoon.

MARGARITA

The Margarita is the world's most ordered cocktail, with blended versions the staple of Tex-Mex restaurants, holiday resorts, and casinos across the globe. This version allows the qualities of the tequila to stand out. You can use Anejo tequilas or Blanco, but I think the softened character of Reposado brings a little sophistication to the drink without losing its agave freshness.

TYPE: SOURS—STRAIGHT UP   **GLASS:**

4 PARTS REPOSADO TEQUILA
2 PARTS COINTREAU
2 PARTS LIME JUICE
GARNISH: SALT RIM,
LIME WEDGE

First salt the rim of the cocktail glass or Margarita coupette. Remove any salt from the inside of the glass; it will quickly dissolve and spoil the drink. Shake the ingredients together with ice and fine-strain into the salt-rimmed, chilled glass. Garnish with a lime wedge.

TAMARIND
MARGARITA

The signature drink of Herradura tequila, this is one of the most delicious drinks I have ever tasted. Tamarind is sweet, sour, savory, and fragranced, and worth the trip to the exotic food store, not only for this drink but also as a fantastic cooking ingredient. The only problem is that it can make the drink look slightly murky brown. If this is an issue, substitute some of the simple syrup for grenadine to make a drink that looks as good as it tastes.

TYPE: SOURS—STRAIGHT UP **GLASS:**

4 PARTS REPOSADO TEQUILA

1.5 PARTS LIME JUICE

1 PART COINTREAU

2 PARTS TAMARIND PULP

1 PART SIMPLE SYRUP

GARNISH: TAJIN OR CHILI LIME SALT (SEE NOTE)

Shake all the ingredients with ice and strain into a chilled glass that has been rimmed with Tajin.

NOTE: Tajin is a brand of chili lime salt, but you can make your own by soaking red chilies in lime juice for 4 hours, then drying them in a very low oven until crisp. Mix with sea salt and grind just like pepper.

REDCURRANT
SOUR

Redcurrants are a strange but natural partner to tequila; their sweet but tart flavor complements the vegetal characteristics of the tequila, making a balanced, refreshing drink. If they are out of season, you can use redcurrant jelly or jam. Use about ¾oz (20g) and reduce the simple syrup to 1 part to make a version that can be drunk all year round.

TYPE: SOURS—ON THE ROCKS   **GLASS:**

1 STRING OF REDCURRANTS
5 PARTS REPOSADO TEQUILA
2.5 PARTS SIMPLE SYRUP
2 PARTS LIME JUICE
1 SMALL EGG WHITE
GARNISH: REDCURRANTS

Muddle the redcurrants in the shaker and then shake all ingredients without ice to emulsify the egg white. Shake again with ice and strain over fresh ice into a large rocks glass. Garnish with a string of redcurrants draped over the rim of the glass.

↻ Swap the tequila for apple brandy or Calvados? Why the hell not!

TEQUILA RASPBERRY
SOUR

A beautiful drink, both to look at and to taste. The tartness of the raspberries is lightened by the frothy, airy egg white, giving a wonderfully velvety texture. If the raspberries are not fully ripe you may need to add an extra dash of syrup. Alternatively, the syrup can be replaced with Chambord raspberry liqueur for an even stronger raspberry flavor.

TYPE: SOURS—STRAIGHT UP   **GLASS:**

5 PARTS REPOSADO TEQUILA
2 PARTS LEMON JUICE
6 FRESH RASPBERRIES
2 PARTS SIMPLE SYRUP
I SMALL EGG WHITE
GARNISH: I RASPBERRY

First shake all the ingredients without ice to emulsify the egg white. Shake again with ice and fine-strain into a chilled cocktail glass. Garnish with a raspberry placed on top of the foam.

PEDRO COLLINS

This drink works with any style of tequila; however, I would probably save my expensive Extra Anejos for shorter drinks, particularly as it is almost impossible to have just one of these! Crisp and refreshing and with no flavors to distract you from the nuances of your chosen tequila—the only thing you need is some sunshine.

TYPE: COLLINS & HIGHBALLS **GLASS:**

5 PARTS TEQUILA
3 PARTS SIMPLE SYRUP
2.5 PARTS LIME JUICE
6 PARTS SODA WATER
GARNISH: LIME WEDGE

Pour the first three ingredients over ice and stir. Top up with soda water and garnish with a lime wedge to allow the drinker to adjust the balance.

JALISCO CRUSH

Apple, tequila, and mint mingle perfectly in this long summer drink. There is no need to muddle the mint, as the flavors will be released during the shake. If you like the clean look of the drink as shown you will need to fine-strain it to remove the mint particles. However, if you leave them in it will taste just as good and can look very pretty.

TYPE: COLLINS & HIGHBALLS   **GLASS:**

5 PARTS TEQUILA
2 PARTS LEMON JUICE
2 PARTS SIMPLE SYRUP
8 MINT LEAVES
6 PARTS PRESSED APPLE JUICE
GARNISH: MINT SPRIG, APPLE WEDGE

Shake all the ingredients with ice and strain into a large highball glass over cracked ice. Garnish with a mint sprig, slapped lightly to release the aroma, and an apple wedge.

♻ Fans of the mojito will love this drink, too, if you use rum rather than tequila.

GRAPEFRUIT
COBBLER

This drink works best if you squeeze the grapefruit juice just before you make it, as the pasteurization process used in cartoned juices ruins the delicate flavors of the grapefruit. Luckily ripe grapefruits yield a lot of juice, so squeezing is not too onerous. This drink also works very well in a punch bowl; keep it cool with a large lump of ice, perhaps with slices of grapefruit frozen inside.

TYPE: COLLINS & HIGHBALLS **GLASS:**

3 SLICES PINK GRAPEFRUIT

5 PARTS TEQUILA

1 PART LEMON JUICE

2 PARTS SIMPLE SYRUP

7 PARTS PINK GRAPEFRUIT JUICE

GARNISH: GRAPEFRUIT SLICE

Muddle the grapefruit slices in a large highball glass, then add the remaining ingredients and some crushed ice. Swizzle and garnish with another slice of pink grapefruit.

Keep the brandy handy here in case all your tequila gets used up for shots.

PALOMA

The Paloma is the national drink of Mexico, where it is made with a brand of sparkling grapefruit soda called Squirt. If you can find this it is great, but if not, the brand Ting, originally from Jamaica, is a good substitute.

TYPE: COLLINS & HIGHBALLS   **GLASS:**

5 PARTS TEQUILA
1.5 PARTS LIME JUICE
9 PARTS SPARKLING GRAPEFRUIT SODA
GARNISH: SEA-SALT RIM, LIME WEDGE

Pour all the ingredients over ice into a large highball glass rimmed with salt. Stir briefly and garnish with a lime wedge.

VELVET VOODOO

Based loosely on the Mai Tai, this drink marries the vanilla notes of Anejo tequila with sweet pineapple and almond, balanced with fresh lime. If you don't have orange Curaçao, Cointreau will work well in this recipe, particularly if you add a dash of orange bitters to the recipe. Be careful: the drink hides its alcohol well, and might leave you slightly bewitched!

TYPE: COLLINS & HIGHBALLS   **GLASS:**

4 PARTS ANEJO TEQUILA
2 PARTS ORANGE CURAÇAO
2 PARTS LIME JUICE
1 PART ORGEAT (ALMOND) SYRUP
5 PARTS PINEAPPLE JUICE
GARNISH: MINT SPRIG, LIME WEDGE,
    CHERRY, PINEAPPLE LEAF (OPTIONAL)

Shake all the ingredients with ice and strain into a large highball glass. Garnish with a lime wedge, mint sprig, cherry, and pineapple leaf (if using).

SOUL HAPPINESS

Making watermelon syrup is really easy—simply push the watermelon flesh through a sieve to obtain the juice and then mix it with equal quantities by weight of superfine (caster) sugar. If you are careful when you remove the flesh you can use the empty shell as a punch bowl—a great idea for a summer party.

TYPE: SOURS—STRAIGHT UP **GLASS:**

5 PARTS REPOSADO TEQUILA
2 PARTS WATERMELON SYRUP
2 PARTS LEMON JUICE
GARNISH: ORANGE TWIST,
WATERMELON WEDGE (OPTIONAL)

Shake all the ingredients with ice and strain into a chilled cocktail glass. Garnish with a large orange twist. If the watermelon is firm enough, cut small wedges to garnish the rim of the glass.

Modify this drink by using brandy rather than tequila.

FALLEN ANGELITA

Halfway between Tommy's Margarita and a classic margarita, this drink was created after a visit to several tequila distilleries. I was trying to recapture the smell of the agua miel—the juice of the cooked agave used in tequila production. This is how I drink my margaritas at home.

TYPE: SOURS—ON THE ROCKS   **GLASS:**

5 PARTS REPOSADO TEQUILA
0.5 PART AGAVE SYRUP
0.5 PART HONEY SYRUP (SEE PAGE 36)
I PART COINTREAU
2 PARTS LIME JUICE
GARNISH: LIME WEDGE

Shake all the ingredients with ice and strain over cubed ice into a large tumbler. Garnish with a lime wedge on the rim so the drinker can adjust the balance if necessary.

TEQUILA ESPRESSO

The Espresso Martini, originally made with vodka, was popularized by the famous English bartender Dick Bradsell in the 1980s; however, it definitely tastes better with tequila! He called it the Pharmaceutical Stimulant, and its pick-me-up effects were not exaggerated. All coffee liqueurs will work here, but Patron XO Café is tailor-made for this drink—it is expensive but worth the treat. If you like your coffee sweet, don't be afraid to add a dash of simple syrup.

TYPE: FLIPS & AFTER DINNER   **GLASS:**

4 PARTS ANEJO TEQUILA

2 PARTS COFFEE LIQUEUR

I SHORT ESPRESSO

GARNISH: 3 COFFEE BEANS

Shake all the ingredients with ice very hard; the espresso will quickly melt the ice. If you're making a large batch you can leave the coffee to cool, but you'll have to shake the ingredients extra hard to froth it up as cold coffee loses its crema. Strain into a chilled cocktail glass and garnish with three coffee beans.

The flavor of coffee is complemented by lots of spirits, including brandy and bourbon.

REDCURRANT
TEQUILA TODDY

Like many countries with hot sun and little rain, Mexico gets surprisingly cold at night. But the party definitely doesn't stop just because the sun has gone down. This drink is the perfect answer—warming, with a heady swirl of fruit, honey, and agave gently steaming from the glass. It also—apparently—has prophylactic properties against colds and flu. I don't know if it works but it is certainly worth trying.

TYPE: HOT DRINKS   **GLASS:**

- I STRING OF REDCURRANTS
- I PART LEMON JUICE
- 2 PARTS ORANGE JUICE
- 5 PARTS CLEAR APPLE JUICE
- 2 PARTS HONEY SYRUP (SEE PAGE 36)
- I PINCH OF GROUND CINNAMON
- 4 PARTS ANEJO TEQUILA

GARNISH: CINNAMON STICK, FRUIT SLICES, REDCURRANTS

Muddle the redcurrants in a saucepan, then add all the other ingredients apart from the tequila. Heat gently until it just begins to simmer, take off the heat, and mix in the tequila. Strain and serve in heatproof glasses. Garnish with a cinnamon stick, lemon and orange slices, and more redcurrants.

Index by cocktail style

General index

Further Reading

The Tequila Ambassador—Tomas Estes
Whisky: The Definitive World Guide to Scotch, Bourbon and Whiskey—
Michael Jackson, Dave Broom, Ian Wisniewski, and Jürgen Deibel
Cognac: A Liquid History—Salvatore Calabrese
Rum: A Global History—Richard Foss
Spirituous Journey: Books 1 and 2: A History of Drink—Jared Brown and
Anistatia Miller
*World's Best Cocktails: 500 Couture Cocktails from the World's Best Bars
and Bartenders*—Tom Sandham
Diffordsguide Cocktails: The Bartender's Bible—Simon Difford
The Essential Cocktail: The Art of Mixing Perfect Drinks—Dale DeGroff

Acknowledgments

I would like to thank, in no particular order:

Fiona and Henry for providing support and distraction in roughly equal
quantities (at least 5 parts of each).

Giles for braving my grumpiness in the office every day for well over a
decade, I hope you enjoy our boozy journey as much as I still do.

Martyn, Dan, and Kevin for your help in all areas of business.

Susan Sowray and William Paul Butt for spawning me and keeping me if
not on, at least close to, the rails.

Pete Jorgensen and his team, without whose patience this would never
have been published. To quote Douglas Adams: "I love deadlines. I love
the whooshing noise they make as they go by."

And finally all the poor inebriated b*****ds who have had to trial all the
drinks in the book generally many, many times. I hope their suffering was
worth it.